KARMA

KARMA

Six Lectures Delivered at
Dornach, Switzerland
February 16 – March 2, 1924

by

Rudolf Steiner

Translated from the original
by Henry B. Monges

THE BOOK TREE
San Diego, California

This authorized English translation
originally printed in agreement with
Harry Collison, M. A. (Oxon.)

© 1943
Anthrposophic Press, Inc.
New York

ISBN 978-1-58509-393-9

Cover art
© Lonely

Cover Layout
Paul Tice

Published by
The Book Tree
P O Box 16476
San Diego, CA 92176
www.thebooktree.com

We provide fascinating and educational products to help awaken the public to new ideas and
information that would not be available otherwise.
Call 1 (800) 700-8733 for our *FREE BOOK TREE CATALOG*.

Preliminary Remarks

We quote the following passages from Rudolf Steiner's *The Story of My Life*. They are to accompany the publication of the lectures which were, in the beginning, privately printed at the urgent wish of the members of the Anthroposophical Society, and now are made accessible to the public in book form.

"From my anthroposophical activity two things have resulted: First my books published for the whole world, and secondly a great number of lecture courses which were at first to be considered as privately printed and to be sold only to members of the Anthroposophical Society. These were really shorthand reports of the lectures more or less well done and which I, for lack of time, could not correct. It would have pleased me best if spoken words had remained spoken words. But the members wished the private publication of the courses. And thus it came into existence. If I had had time to correct the reports, the restriction 'For Members Only' would never have been necessary. For more than a year now, this restriction has been removed.

"Here, in this *Story of My Life*, it is necessary to say, first of all, how the two things—my published books and this privately printed matter—fit into that which I elaborated as anthroposophy.

"Whoever wishes to trace my inner struggle and labor to set anthroposophy before the consciousness of the present age must do this on the basis of the writings published for general circulation. In these I dealt also with all which is present in the striving of this age for knowledge. Here there is given what more and more took form for me in 'spiritual perception,' what became the structure of anthroposophy—in a form incomplete, to be sure, from many points of view.

"Together with this purpose, however, of building up anthroposophy and thereby serving only that which results when one has information from the world of spirit to give to the modern culture world, there now appeared the other demand—to meet fully whatever was manifested in the membership as the need of their souls, as their longing for the spirit.

"Most of all was there a strong inclination to hear the Gospels and the biblical writings generally set forth in that which had appeared as the anthroposophic light. Persons wished to attend courses of lectures on these revelations given to mankind.

"As private courses of lectures were held in the sense then required, something else arose in consequence. Only members attended these courses. These members were acquainted with the elementary information coming from anthroposophy. It was possible to speak to them as to persons advanced in the realm of anthroposophy. The manner of these private lectures was such as it would not have been in writings intended wholly for the public.

"In private groups I was allowed to speak about things in a manner which I should have been obliged to shape quite differently for a public presentation if, from the first, these things had been designed for such an audience.

"Thus in the two things, the public and the private writings, we have really something derived from two different bases. All the public writings are the result of what struggled and labored within me; in the privately printed matter the Society itself shares in the struggle and labor. I listen to the vibrations in the soul-life of the membership, and through my vital living within what I thus hear the bearing of the course is determined.

"Because of this working out of the reality of the members' soul-needs, the privately printed matter *must* be judged differently from that given to the public from the beginning. The content of this printed matter was originally intended as oral, not printed, information. The subjects discussed were determined by the soul-needs of the members as these needs appeared with the passage of time.

"What is contained in the published writings corresponds to the demands of anthroposophy as such; in the manner in which the private printed matter evolved, the configuration of soul of the whole Society has co-operated."

KARMA

I

Dornach, February 16, 1924

My dear Friends:

I SHOULD like to begin by speaking to you about the conditions and laws underlying human destiny, destiny, which customarily is called karma. This karma, however, will be understood, be clearly seen into only when we begin by acquainting ourselves with the varieties of laws underlying the universe. So today, then, I should like—for it is necessary—to speak to you in a rather abstract form about the various underlying universal laws, in order then to crystallize out of this the more special form which can be designated as human destiny—*karma*.

We speak of cause and effect not only when we wish to comprehend the phenomena of the world, but also when we wish to fix our attention on the phenomena of human life itself. And at present it is quite customary to speak in general terms about cause and effect. Especially is this so in scientific circles. However, directly from this there result the greatest difficulties concerning the actual truth. For the various ways in which cause and effect appear in the world are not at all considered.

We can begin by looking at the so-called lifeless nature which, indeed, confronts us most clearly in the mineral kingdom, in all that we see in the rocky and stony part of the earth, often in such wonderful formations, but also in all that is reduced to powder and which is then reunited and repacked in the formless rocky strata of the earth. Let us look, my dear friends, first at what thus appears as the lifeless in the world.

When we consider the lifeless—everything lifeless, without exception—we discover that everywhere within this kingdom of the lifeless we can find the causes themselves. Wherever the lifeless exists as effect, we can also seek the causes within this very same kingdom. In fact, we proceed in accordance with the principles of knowledge only when we seek the causes of the processes of the lifeless within its own kingdom.

If you have a crystal before you, however beautifully formed it may be, you should seek the cause of its forms in the kingdom of the lifeless itself. And thus this lifeless kingdom shows itself as something contained within itself. We are, at first, not able to say where we can find the limits of this lifeless. Under certain conditions they may lie far distant out in the reaches of the universe. But if we are concerned with the effects of something lifeless confronting us, and we wish to find the causes, we must then seek them also within the realm of the lifeless. Through what we have said, however, we have already placed the lifeless alongside something else, and therewith a certain perspective is immediately opened before us.

Consider the human being himself. Consider how he passes through the door of death. Everything which existed and acted in him before this event has left the visible, apprehensible form which remains after the human soul has passed through death's portal; nothing remains but this discarded, deserted form, of which we say that it is lifeless. And just as we speak of the lifeless when we gaze upon the stony structure of the mountains with its crystal forms, so must we speak of the lifeless when we behold this human corpse, bereft of soul and spirit. What from the beginning prevailed in the rest of lifeless nature only now comes into existence for the corpse of the human being.

We were unable to find in the lifeless itself the causes of what occurs in the human form as effects during life before the soul has passed through the door of death. It is true that, when an arm is raised, not only do we seek in vain in the lifeless, physical laws of the human form for the cause of this action, but we shall also seek in vain in the realm of the chemical, in the realm of the physical forces which are present in the human form, for the cause, let us say, of the heart-beat, of the blood circulation, of any of the processes which are not at all under the control of the will.

But, at the moment when the human form has become a corpse, when the soul has stepped through the gateway of death, we observe an effect in the human organism. We perceive, let us say, a change in the color of the skin, the limbs become limp; briefly, everything appears which we are accustomed to behold in a corpse. Where do we seek the cause? In the corpse itself, in the chemical, physical, lifeless forces of the corpse itself.

When now in all its aspects, in all directions, you think out to the end what I have here indicated—I need only indicate it—you will realize that, after the human soul has crossed the threshold of death, the human being has then become, regarding his corpse, like lifeless nature about him. That means that we must now seek the causes for the effects in the same region in which the effects themselves lie. This is very important.

As soon, however, as we behold this special nature of the human corpse, we find something else that is extraordinarily significant. The human being casts off his corpse, as it were, at death. And if then, with that faculty of perception which is capable of it, we observe what the real human being, the soul-spirit human being, has become after he has passed through the door of death, we are compelled to say: Indeed, it is quite true that the corpse is cast off, and that now it has no longer any significance for this actual soul-spirit human being, who has reached the other side of death's door. This corpse has no longer any significance; it is now something discarded.

With lifeless external nature this is quite a different matter. And, indeed, even if we consider the matter only superficially, this difference confronts us. Let us observe a human corpse. It can best be observed where it has had an air-burial. In subterranean caves, which formerly were chiefly used by certain communities as burial places, we find the corpses of men, for example, simply hung up. There they dry out. They go so far in this drying out process and become so completely brittle that it only requires a little tap to cause them to fall into dust.

What we thus find preserved as the lifeless is something quite different from what we find outside in our earthly surroundings as lifeless nature. This lifeless nature fashions itself, it forms itself into crystal shapes. It is in a remarkable state of change. When we disregard what is purely earthly and look at other phenomena which are also lifeless, at water, and air, we then find that an active transformation and metamorphosis takes place in these lifeless elements. Let us now place this before the soul. Let us bear in mind the similarity of the human body in its lifelessness, after the soul has laid it aside, to extra-human lifeless nature.

Let us now proceed further. Let us consider the plant kingdom. Here we enter the sphere of the living. If we study a plant intimately, we shall never find ourselves able to explain the effect appearing in the plant merely as a result of the causes which lie in the plant kingdom itself—that is, in the same kingdom in which the effects appear. Certainly, there is today a science which attempts to do this. However, this science is on the wrong track, for finally it comes to the point of saying: Yes, indeed, it is possible to investigate the physical forces and laws acting in the plant; the chemically active forces and laws can be investigated; but something remains over and above. At this point these people divide into two groups. One group maintains that what remains over is only a sort of aggregation, a sort of form, shape; that what is active are only the physical and chemical laws. The other group says: No! there is something else there besides, which science has not yet investigated; science will, however, eventually discover it. But this will be said for a long time to come. The fact of the matter, however, is something different. For, when we wish to investigate plant nature, we cannot comprehend it, if the entire universe is not called to our aid, if the plant is not beheld in such a way that we say that the forces of plant activity lie in the reaches of the cosmos. Everything that happens in the plant is the effect of the reaches of the universe. The sun must first advance to a certain position in the cosmos in order that some particular effects may appear in the plant kingdom. Different forces must be active from wide spaces of the universe in order that the plant may receive its form, in order that it may receive its inner driving forces.

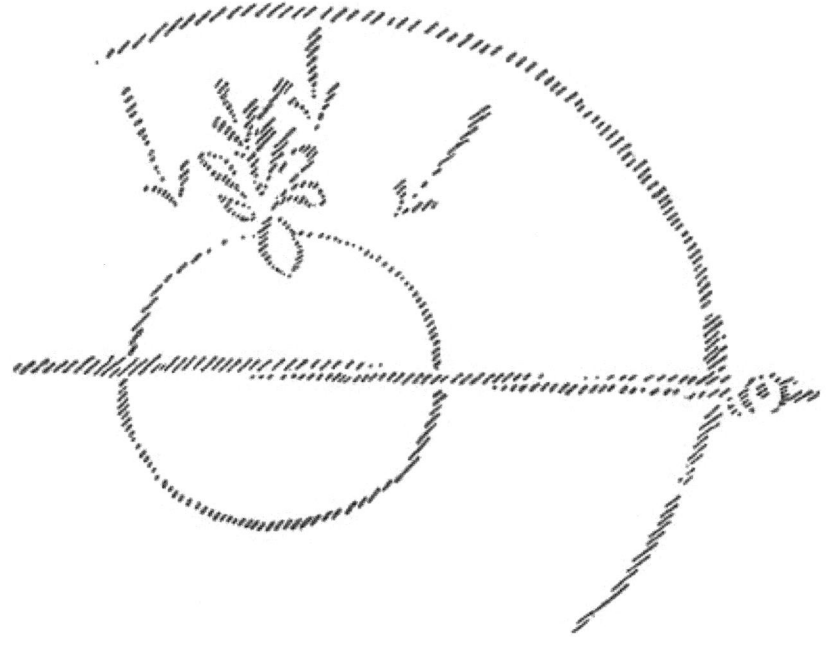

Figure I

My dear friends, the truth of the matter is as follows. If we were able to travel, not in the manner of Jules Verne, but actually to travel out to the moon, to the sun, etc., then, unless we should have already acquired other forces of cognition than those we now possess, we would not become any more clever in this search for the causes than we are upon the earth itself. We would not get very far were we to say the following: "Very well, the causes of the effects which appear in the plant kingdom are not in the plant kingdom of the earth itself; so we travel to the sun; we shall find there the causes." But we do not find them there with ordinary means of cognition. We do find them, however, if we lift ourselves to imaginative knowledge, if we possess quite a different mode of knowledge. In that case we do not need to travel to the sun; we find them here in the earth region itself. Only we shall find it necessary to cross over from an ordinary physical world to an ether world, and we shall find that in the reaches of the world the cosmic ether works everywhere with its forces, and that out of these reaches it works inward. Out of cosmic reaches everywhere the ether forces work into our world.

Thus we must actually cross over to a second kingdom of the world, if we intend to seek the causes of the effects in the plant kingdom.

Now, the human being participates in the same element as the plant. The same forces which send their influences from the reaches of the ether cosmos down into the plants work also in the human being. He carries within him the ether forces, and we designate the sum of the forces he thus carries the ether body. And I have already told you how this ether body a few days after death becomes larger and larger and finally loses itself, so that the human being remains only in his astral and ego being. Thus what he has carried within him of an etheric nature becomes larger and larger and finally loses itself in the cosmic reaches.

Let us now compare again what we can see of the human being when he has crossed the threshold of death with what we see in the plant kingdom. We must say that the causative forces of the plant kingdom come down to earth out of the reaches of space. We must say in regard to the human ether body that the forces of this ether body go out into these reaches, that is to say, they go to that region whence come the growth forces of the plant when the human being has passed through death's door. Now the matter already becomes clearer. If we merely look at a physical corpse and say that it is lifeless, then a descent into the rest of lifeless nature becomes difficult for us. But, if we look at the living, at the plant kingdom, and become aware that the causative forces for this kingdom come out of the cosmic reaches, then by plunging ourselves imaginatively into the nature of man, we see that, when the human being has crossed the threshold of death, the human ether body goes out into the source whence come the etheric forces of the plant kingdom.

Something else, however, is characteristic. What acts upon the plants as causative forces, acts relatively quickly; for upon the plants which are springing from the ground, which are developing their blossoms and their fruit, the sun of the day before yesterday has but little influence today. The sun of the day before yesterday is not effecting very much as a causative force. The sun must shine today, really shine today. That is important. And you will notice in our subsequent considerations that it is important that we note this fact.

The plants with their ether-causative forces have, it is true, their actual fundamental forces within the realm of the earthly, but they have these in what exists simultaneously in the cosmos and the earth. And when the human ether body dissolves itself, after the human being as a soul-spirit being has passed through the portal of death, this process lasts only a brief time, a few days only. Again a simultaneous relationship exists, for the days during which this dissolution takes place, measured in the time of cosmic events, are but an insignificant moment.

When the ether body returns to that region whence come the ether forces which manifest as plant growth forces, we have, again, to do with something which shows us that as soon as the human being lives in the ether, his ether activity is not limited to the earth, for it departs from the earth, yet it develops with simultaneousness.

I shall now tabulate the foregoing in the following manner. We can say:

Mineral Kingdom: Simultaneousness of cause and effect in the physical.

Thus we have essentially to do with simultaneousness of the causes in the physical. You will say: "Yes, but the causes of much that occurs in the physical lie prior in time." This is in reality not the fact. If effects are to arise in the physical, then the causes must last, must continue to act. If the causes cease, effects no longer occur. We are, therefore, justified in writing this down thus:

Mineral Kingdom: Simultaneousness of the causes in the physical.

When we come to the plant kingdom, however—and in doing so we come to what can be observed in the human being also as something plantlike—we then have to do with simultaneousness in the physical and the super-physical.

Plant Kingdom: Simultaneousness of the causes in the physical and super-physical.

Let us now approach the animal kingdom. In this kingdom we shall seek quite in vain in the animal itself for what appears as effects as long as the animal is living. Even if the animal only crawls in order to seek its food, we shall seek quite in vain for the causes in the chemical and physical processes taking place within the animal body. We shall also seek entirely in vain in the reaches of ether space, where we find the causes for the plant nature,—we shall also seek there in vain for the causes of animal movement and animal sensation. For all that takes place in the animal in regard to what is plantlike in the animal, we find the causes also in ether space. And when the animal dies, its ether body also passes out into the reaches of cosmic ether. But we shall never be able to find within the earthly, within the physical, or the super-physical etheric, the causes of sensation. It is impossible to find them there.

Here it can be said that something occurs wherein the modern view is very much on the wrong track. Indeed, in regard to many phenomena which appear in the animal—the phenomena of sensation, of movement—the human being with this modern conception must say to himself: "If I investigate the inner processes of the animal's physical, chemical forces, I cannot find the causes there. But also in the reaches of the cosmos, in the ether reaches of the universe the causes cannot be found. If I wish to explain the nature of a blossom, then I must go out into the ether universe. I shall be able to explain the blossom's nature from the nature of the ether universe. I shall also be able to explain much in the animal which is plantlike from the nature of the ether cosmos, but I shall never be able to explain what appears in the animal as movement or as sensation."

If I observe an animal on the 20th of June and consider its sensations, then I shall not be able to find the causes of the sensations on the 20th of June in anything that is in earthly or extra-earthly space. If I go still farther back I shall not find them either. I shall not find them in May, nor in April, nor in any other month.

The modern view feels this. Therefore this modern view explains what is thus not capable of explanation, or at least a great deal of it, by means of heredity. That is to say, it explains by means of a phrase. *It is "inherited."* It originates with the forebears, it is "inherited" by the offspring. Naturally, not everything, because that would, indeed, be too grotesque; nevertheless, a great deal. It is inherited!

What is meant by "inherited"? The concept of heredity leads finally back to the idea that what appears as complicated animal was contained in its mother's ovum. And it has, indeed, been the endeavor of the modern view to observe an ox outwardly in its complicated form and then to say: "Well, the ox sprang from the ovum; in it were the forces which then resulted in the fullgrown ox. Therefore, the ovum is an extraordinarily complicated body."

It would have to be extremely complicated, this ovum of the cow, for, is it not true? everything is contained within it which presses toward all sides, and forms, and fashions, and works, in order that out of the little ovum the complicated ox may emerge!

And however much we may struggle to find a way out—there are, indeed, many theories of evolution, of epigenesis, etc.—whatever way out we try to find, we see that there is nothing else to do than to conclude that this ovum, this little egg, is something extremely complicated. Since everything is led back to the molecule, which is built up of atoms in a complicated way, there are many who represent the first inception of this ovum as a complicated molecule. But, my dear friends, this does not even agree with physical observations.

The question arises: Is this ovum really such a complicated molecule, already such a complicated organism? The peculiarity of the ovum does not at all consist in its complexity, but in the fact that it throws all its substance back into chaos—into a chaotic state. Precisely the ovum is, in the mother-animal, not a complicated structure, but a completely pulverized, disarranged substance. It is not organized at all. It is something that falls back into an absolutely unorganized, powderlike condition. And reproduction would never occur, did not the unorganized, the lifeless matter—which tends toward the crystalline, toward the form—did not this matter in the ovum fall back into itself, into chaos. The albumen is not the most complicated body, but rather the simplest, which has nothing determinative in it. And out of this little chaos, which exists there at first as an ovum, no ox could ever come into existence, for this ovum is just a chaos. Why, then, does an ox come forth from it? Because, in the maternal organism, the entire cosmos acts upon this ovum. It is just because it is unconditioned, because it is chaotic, that the entire cosmos can act upon it. And fructification has no other purpose than to cast back the matter of the ovum into chaos, into the indeterminate, into the unconditioned. Thus, nothing else acts but the universe alone.

But now, if we look into the mother, we do not find therein the causes.

If we look outside into the ether world, there also in the simultaneous occurrences the causes are not to be found. We must go back until we come to the time before the animal was born, if we wish to find the causes for what germinates there as the potential capacities of a being, capable of sensation and movement. We must go back to a time before life has begun. That is, for the capacities of feeling and movement the causal world does not lie in simultaneousness, but lies in a time prior to the conception of this being.

The following is the curious fact: If I behold a plant, I must go out into what is simultaneous, and I then find the cause; but I find it in the reaches of the universe. If, however, I wish to find the cause of what acts in the animal as sensation, then I cannot look for it in simultaneousness, but I must look for it in what preceded life; in other words, the stellar constellation must have changed, it must have become different. It is not the stellar constellation in the universe which exists simultaneously with the animal that has its influence upon the actual animal nature, but the constellation of the stars preceding its life.

And now let us look at the human being when he has passed the threshold of death. When this has occurred he must go back—after he has laid aside his ether body, which spreads out into every part of the reaches of the universe from whence come the growth forces of the plants, the etheric forces—he must go back, as I have described it, to his moment of birth. Then he has experienced in his astral body all that he has gone through in life, but in reverse order. In other words, the human being must not pass into the state of simultaneousness with his astral body after death; he must go back to the state prior to birth. He must go to that region whence come the forces which give the animal the capacity for sensation and the ability of movement. These do not come out of simultaneously existing stellar constellations, they come from the constellations existing prior to birth.

Thus, if we speak of the animal kingdom, we cannot speak of the simultaneousness of the causes in the physical and superphysical, but we must then speak of past super-physical causes passing over to the present effects in the physical.

Animal Kingdom: Past superphysical causes to present effects.

And here, too, we enter again the concept of time. We must, if I may use a trivial expression, go for a walk in time. If we wish to seek the causes of something occurring in the physical world, we go for a walk in this world; we do not need to go outside the physical world. If we wish to seek the causes of something which is really in the living plant kingdom, then we must go quite far away. We must seek in the ether world. And only there where the ether world comes to an end, where—speaking in terms of a fairy tale—the world is fenced, is boarded in, there only do we find the causes of plant growth.

We may go about there as much as we wish, yet we shall not find the cause of the faculty of sensation or movement. We must begin to go for a walk in time, we must tread there the path of time in reverse order. We must leave space and go for a walk in time.

You will note that we can place the human physical body in its lifelessness alongside lifeless outer nature in respect of causation; we can place the human ether body in its life and its expansion after death into the ether spaces alongside the ether life of the plant, which also comes hither out of the reaches of the ether, but, indeed, out of the simultaneous constellations of the superphysical, of the super-earthly. And we are able to place the human astral organism alongside of that which exists outside in the animal nature.

And we then advance from the mineral, to the plant, to the animal kingdom, coming finally to the real human kingdom. You will say: "Well, we have already considered that from the beginning." Yes, indeed, but not altogether. We have, in the first place, considered the human kingdom in so far as the human being has a physical body; then, in so far as he has an ether body, and then, in so far as he has an astral body. But just note that he would be a crystal—a complicated one, to be sure, but a crystal, nevertheless—if he had only his physical body. If he were to have merely his ether body in addition, he would then be a plant, a beautiful plant perhaps, nevertheless, just a plant. If, again, the human being had in addition an astral body, he would go about on all fours, perhaps have horns and other similar animal characteristics—in short, he would be just an animal. The human being is none of these. The form which he has as an erect walking being he has by virtue of his possessing an ego organism besides the physical, etheric, and astral organisms. And only this being, who also has an ego organism, can we designate as man, as belonging to the human kingdom.

Let us now once more consider what we have already observed. If we wish to seek the causes of plant nature, we must then go out into the reaches of the ether realm, but we are still able to remain in space; only, as has been remarked, space in that case becomes somewhat hypothetical, for we must even resort to the fairy-tale concept, we must go "where the world is boarded up." It is, however, really a fact that even modern human beings who think in accord with purely natural scientific research are coming to the view that we can actually speak of something like that expressed in the fairy tale "where the world is boarded in." It is, naturally, a trivial, clumsy expression. But we need only recall how childishly human beings think: There is the sun. It sends forth its rays, sends them farther and farther away. They become, it is true, weaker and weaker. The light goes on and on and on, it goes further and further away, into the endless.

I have explained long ago to those who have already for years heard my lectures that it is nonsense to imagine that the light goes out into the endless. I have always said that the outspreading of light is dependent on its elasticity. If we take a rubber ball and depress it, we can do this only up to a certain point, it then snaps back again. That is to say, the elasticity of the ball has its limits; then the depressed surface springs back into place. This I have said is also true of light. It does not go out into the limitless, but, when a certain limit is reached, it returns.

This fact, that light does not expand out into the boundless, but only to a certain limit and then comes back, has found an advocate, for example, in England in the physicist Sir Oliver Lodge. So it can be seen that today physical science has already come to advocate what is given through spiritual science, and physical science will eventually accept, in all particulars, what is stated by spiritual science.

And thus it is, indeed, possible to speak also of the fact that there outside, if we think sufficiently far out into space, we must allow our thoughts to return and not permit ourselves simply to postulate endless space, which is fantastic—indeed, a fantasy we cannot imagine. Perhaps there may be some among you who will remember that in the description of the course of my life I said how very deep an impression was made on me when, in my study of modern synthetic geometry, I was led to the concept that a straight line may not be considered as having a limitless extension, a never ending extension, but that such a line extending in one direction actually returns from the other. Geometry expresses it somewhat as follows: The point at infinity to the right of a fixed point is the same as the infinitely distant point to the left. It is possible to calculate this. This is not merely analogous to the fact that when we have a circle and start here by following the circumference we return to the same point again, or that, if a semicircle is infinite it is a straight line. That is not the case. That would be an analogy to which those who can think with exactness do not attribute any value. What made an impression on me was not this trivial analogy, but the actual proof in accordance with strict calculation, that the infinitely distant point on the left is the same as the infinitely distant point on the right, and that actually if some one begins to run from here along a straight line continually he will not run to a limitless infinity, but that, if he but continue to run for the proper length of time, he will eventually come toward us again from the opposite direction. This appears grotesque to all physical thought. The moment physical thinking is laid aside, this is actually a reality, because the universe is not endless, but is limited in as far as the physical universe is concerned. Thus it may be said that we reach the limits of the etheric when we speak of the vegetative and of what is etheric in the human being. But we must go outside of everything that exists in space when we wish to explain the animal and the astral nature in man. There we must go walking in time; there we must go beyond simultaneousness; there we must advance in time.

When we enter time we cross the boundary of the physical in a twofold way. In describing the animal we must already proceed in time. We must, however, not continue this mode of thinking abstractly, but continue it in a concrete way. Pay attention for a moment and see how this can be continued concretely.

Human beings think, do they not? that when the sun sends forth its light, this continues on its path endlessly. Sir Oliver Lodge shows, however, that we have already forsaken this mode of thinking about the matter and, instead, that we know that light comes to a boundary and then returns again. The sun receives back its light from all sides, although in another form, in a transformed condition. The sun receives back the light. Let us now employ this mode of thinking on what we have just been considering. We stand, at the outset, in space. Earth-space remains within it. We stride out into the universe. That is not yet enough for us: we stride out into time. Now some one could say: "Very well, we now stride on ever further and further." No, not at all! We now return again. We must continue this mode of thinking. We return again. We come back again in the same way as we do when we march forth into space, going ever further, reaching finally the boundary, and then return. So here also do we return. That is to say, if we have sought the past superphysical causes in the reaches of time, we must return again into the physical.

What does that mean? It means, we must again descend out of time, out of time descend again upon the earth. If we wish, thus, to seek the causes of the human being, then we must seek them again upon earth. Now we have marched back in time. If, by marching back in time, we come again upon the earth, then of course we come into a previous human life. With the animal, we stride further; it dissipates in regard to time just as our ether body dissipates right out to the boundary of the cosmos. The human being does not dissipate himself out there, for when we retrace his path in time we come back to the earth into his previous life. Thus we must say for the human being: From past physical causes to present effects in the physical.

> *Mineral Kingdom:* Simultaneousness of causes in the physical.
> *Plant Kingdom:* Simultaneousness of the causes in the physical and super-physical.
> *Animal Kingdom:* Past super-physical causes of present effects.
> *Human Kingdom:* Past physical causes of present effects in the physical.

You see, it has required effort today to familiarize ourselves with abstractions in a preparatory way. But that, my dear friends, was necessary. It was necessary, because I wished to show you that there is also a logic for those spheres which we must consider to be the spiritual. Only, this logic does not agree with the clumsy logic which is deduced merely from physical phenomena, and in which human beings are accustomed entirely and only to believe.

If we proceed in a purely logical way and investigate the series of causes, then, in the mere train of thought, we reach the past earth lives. And it is necessary to call attention to the fact that also the mode of thinking itself must become different from the usual mode, if we wish to comprehend the spiritual.

Human beings believe that what reveals itself from the spiritual world cannot be comprehended. It can be comprehended, but we must broaden our logic. It is, indeed, also necessary, if we wish to comprehend a musical or any other work of art, that we bear in ourselves the conditions which meet the matter halfway. If we do not possess these conditions then we understand nothing concerning them. Then the music passes us by as a noise. Or we may see in some work of art nothing but an incomprehensible shape. Thus we must also meet what is communicated from the spirit world with a mode of thought commensurate with this world. This, however, becomes evident in mere logical thinking. By investigating the various natures of the causes, we reach, indeed, the possibility of understanding the past earth lives also in logical sequence.

Now there remains the important question, which begins there where we observe the corpse. It has become lifeless. Lifeless nature exists outside in its crystal forms, in its varied shapes. The important question now confronts us: What is the relationship of lifeless nature to the corpse of the human being?

Perhaps you will see, my dear friends, that something is being contributed to a meaning which lies in the direction of the answer to this question, if you take hold of the matter in its second step, if you say: When I behold the plant world surrounding me, then I realize that it carries in itself the forces coming from the reaches of the ether cosmos to which my ether body returns. There outside in the ether reaches, there above are the causative sources of the plants. Thither goes my ether body when it has served its purpose during my life. I go thither where plant life gushes forth from the ether reaches. I go thither—that is, I am related to it. Indeed, I can say: Something exists there above me; my ether body ascends to it; the verduring, sprouting, up-springing plant world comes thither from it. But there is a difference. I give up my ether body; the plants receive the ether in order to grow. They receive the ether in order to live. I yield up the ether body after death. I yield it up as something remaining over. The plants, however, receive this ether body as something that gives them life. They have their beginning in that region which I reach at my end. The plant beginning unites with the human ether body's ending.

May it perhaps be that in relation to the mineral, to the crystals of the most manifold forms, I can ask the following question: Is that which I leave behind as physical corpse, as an end of myself, perhaps also a beginning of the mineral? Do beginning and end perhaps meet?

With this question in mind we intend to close today, my dear friends, and to begin tomorrow, in order to enter thoroughly into the question of human destiny, of so-called karma. Thus, in the next lecture, I shall continue to speak about karma. You will then no longer have to find your way through such a thicket of abstractions, but you will also understand that this was quite necessary for a certain development of thought.

II

Dornach, February 17, 1924

WHEN we advance from the study the aim of which was to prepare us for the explanation of human destiny, of karma, when we advance from abstractions, from the intellectual, to life itself, this advance then brings us, first of all, to the point of placing before our minds the various spheres of life into which the human being is inserted, in order to gain from these constituents of life a basis for a characterization of karma, of human destiny.

Indeed, the human being belongs to the whole cosmos in a much more comprehensive sense than is usually thought. He is, indeed, a member of the cosmos, and without the cosmos he is nothing. I have often employed the comparison of some human bodily member, for example, a finger: A finger is a finger by virtue of its being a part of the human organism. The moment it is severed from the human organism it is no longer a finger. Outwardly, physically, as finger it is the same as previously, but after it has been severed from the human organism it is, indeed, no longer a finger. In like manner is the human being no longer a human being when he is lifted out of the general cosmic existence. He belongs to the general cosmic existence, and without it he cannot at all be looked upon, not at all be comprehended as a human being.

As we have already seen from yesterday's lecture, the world surroundings of mankind consist of various domains. To begin with, we have the lifeless domain of the world which, in ordinary language, we call the domain of the mineral world. We become similar to this domain of the mineral world as the lifeless element only after we have laid aside our body, when we, as far as this body is concerned, have passed through the portal of death. In our real being we never become similar to this lifeless element. The discarded bodily form alone becomes similar to this element.

Thus we have on the one hand what the human being leaves behind as a physical corpse in the realm of the lifeless, and, on the other, what exists as the widespread lifeless, crystalline and non-crystalline mineral nature and world. As human beings we are entirely dissimilar to this mineral world as long as we live upon the earth. To this I have already drawn attention. In regard to our form, we are immediately destroyed when we are consigned to the mineral world as a corpse. We disintegrate into the mineral; that is, the element which holds our form together has nothing in common with mineral nature. From this it follows that the human being as he lives in the physical world cannot be actually influenced at all by the mineral nature itself.

The chief and most comprehensive influences which act upon the human being from the mineral kingdom come in a roundabout way through the senses. We see the mineral kingdom, we hear it, we perceive its warmth, briefly, we perceive it by means of the senses. Our other relationships to the mineral nature are extremely slight. Just consider how very little of a mineral nature enters into relationship with us during earth life. The salt with which we flavor our food is mineral, and a few other things which we take in with our food are of a mineral nature, but by far the largest part of the food stuff which the human being consumes comes from the plant and animal kingdoms. And what we receive from the mineral kingdom relates itself in a very peculiar way to what we receive from the mineral world through our senses simply as soul impressions, as sense perceptions. And I beg you to consider seriously in this connection something very important. I have, indeed, frequently described this: The human brain weighs on the average about 1500 grams. This is quite a weight. The blood vessels at the base of this brain would be completely crushed by it if they were so heavily pressed upon by such a weight as this. But the brain does not press so heavily, for it is subject to a certain law. This law, which I have described here recently, says that an object immersed in a liquid loses some of its weight.

This can be shown by experiment, by taking a pair of scales—first disregarding the liquid-filled vessel—weighing this object, and noting its weight. Then place the vessel containing the water underneath one of the scale pans so that the object in the scale pan sinks into the water. Immediately the scale pans are no longer in balance. The pan containing the weight drops lower, because the object in the other pan becomes lighter. If you then investigate how much lighter the object in question becomes, you will find that it is lighter by an amount equal to the weight of the fluid which the object displaces. If thus you take water as a fluid, then will the weight of the body immersed be reduced by an amount equal to the weight of the displaced water. This is the so-called principle of Archimedes. He discovered this—as I have told you on another occasion—when taking a bath. By simply sitting in the bath he found that his leg became lighter or heavier, according as he inserted it in the water or lifted it out again. And he then cried: I have found it! Eureka!

Indeed, my dear friends, what has just been said is an extremely important fact; important facts, however, are often forgotten. Had the engineering art not forgotten this Archimedean principle, then in Italy perhaps one of the greatest disasters of recent times would not have occurred. These are just the things which occur also in outer life from inability to survey clearly present-day knowledge.

In any case, the body loses in weight an amount equal to the weight of the displaced water. Now, the brain is completely immersed in the cerebral fluid. It swims within this brain water. Once in a while, at the present time, the human being comes to realize that in so far as he is solid, he is actually a fish. In reality he is, indeed, a fish, for 90% of his body consists of water and the solid element swims within it like the fish in water.

Thus the brain by swimming in the cerebral fluid becomes so much lighter than formerly that it weighs only 20 grams. The brain which out of its fluid weighs some 1500 grams, in its fluid presses upon its base with a weight of only 20 grams. Now just consider how strong in us is the tendency in such an important organ—on account of this swimming of our brain in the cerebral fluid—the tendency to become free from the earth. We do not at all think with an organ which is subject to the influence of gravity, but rather we think in opposition to this force of gravity. The brain organ has first been relieved of the force of gravity.

If you consider the wide significance of the impressions which you receive through the senses, and which you confront with your free will, and compare this with the minute influences which come from salt and similar substances absorbed as food or seasoning, then the following will result from your observation: So great is the predominance of our mere sense impressions, which render us independent of the stimuli from the mineral kingdom, that what we receive into ourselves as direct influence from the mineral world is related to our sense perceptions in the ratio of 20 to 1500 grams. What we take into ourselves through the sense perceptions does not tear us apart, and the elements in us which actually are subject to the earth's gravity—such as the mineral seasonings in our food—are, for the most part, things that conserve us inwardly; for salt has at the same time a conserving, a maintaining, a refreshing force. The human being is thus, on the whole, independent of what exists in the surrounding mineral kingdom. He takes into himself from the mineral kingdom only that which has no direct influence on his inner nature. He moves about freely and independently in the mineral world.

My dear friends, if this freedom and independence of movement in the mineral world did not exist, what we call human freedom would not exist at all. And it is very important that we must acknowledge that the mineral kingdom actually exists as the necessary counterpart of human freedom. Indeed, were there no mineral kingdom, we would not be free beings. For the moment we ascend into the plant kingdom, we are no longer independent of that kingdom. It only seems as if we directed our eyes toward the plant kingdom in just the same way we direct them toward the crystal, toward the widespread mineral kingdom. That is, however, not the case. Here, on the earth, the plant kingdom lies outspread. And we human beings are born into the world as breathing, living beings, as beings having a certain metabolism. All this is, indeed, much more dependent on the environment than our eyes, our ears, than everything that is a transmitter of sense impressions. What exists as plant world, the outspread plant world, draws its life out of the strength-giving ether pouring from all sides downward into the earth. The human being also is subject to this ether.

When we are born as a little child and begin to grow, when the forces of growth are evident in us, these are the ether forces. The same forces which cause the plants to grow live in us as ether forces. We carry within us the ether body. The physical body harbors our eyes, harbors our ears. As I have just explained, this body has nothing in common with the rest of the physical world, and what shows this to be true is the fact that, as a corpse, it decays in the physical world.

In the case of the ether body we have at once a different condition. Through this ether body we are related to the plant kingdom. But by our growing—just consider this, my dear friends—by virtue of our growing, something forms itself within us which has a deep connection, in a certain sense, with our destiny. To employ some rather grotesque, radical illustrations, we may grow and yet remain small and fat, or become tall and slim; we may grow and have this or that shape of nose. In brief, the way we grow has most decidedly a certain influence upon our external appearance. This, again, is connected—although in the first place only loosely—with our destiny. Growth does not express itself, however, only in these coarser things. Were the instruments we possess for purposes of research fine enough, we should discover that actually every human being has a different liver composition, a different spleen composition, a different brain composition. Liver is not merely liver. In every individual—naturally, in a very delicate way—it is something different. All this is connected with the same forces which cause the plants to grow. And in beholding the plant cover of the earth we must become conscious of the fact that what pours in out of the reaches of the ether, causing the plants to grow, works and acts also in us; it produces in us the original human potentiality which has a great deal to do with our destiny. For whether a person has received this or that liver, lung, or brain composition from the etheric universe is a matter profoundly connected with his destiny.

We see only the outer side, to be sure, of all these things. Certainly, if we look upon the mineral kingdom, we see about all that exists in that world. Human beings are so fond, scientifically, of this mineral world—if it is at all possible to speak of a "scientific fondness" at the present time—because it contains everything that people wish to find.

This is certainly not the case with what sustains, as forces, the plant kingdom. For the moment we attain imaginative knowledge—I have already spoken of this on other occasions—we begin immediately to see that the minerals are of such a nature that they are enclosed in the mineral kingdom. What sustains the plant kingdom does not appear externally at all to ordinary consciousness. Here we must penetrate deeper into the world.

Suppose we ask the question: What is it really that acts in the plant kingdom? What acts there so that there can come from the distant ether reaches the forces which make the plants sprout and spring forth from the earth, which also cause our growth, however, and the finer composition of our whole body,—what acts there? This question then brings us to the beings of the so-called third Hierarchy, the Angeloi, Archangeloi, and Archai. These beings are the realm of the invisible; but without them there would be no up and down surging of the ether forces which cause the plants to grow, and which act in us through our having within us the same forces that cause growth in plants. We can no longer stop at the mere visible—unless we wish to remain dull in regard to knowledge—if we approach the plant world and its forces. And we must, indeed, become conscious of the fact that in the body-free existence between death and a new birth we develop our relationships, our connections with these beings, the Angeloi, Archangeloi, and Archai. And according to the way we develop these connections and relationships with these beings of the third

Hierarchy, does the karma of our inner nature—if I may designate it thus—fashion itself, that very karma which depends upon the way our ether body combines the bodily fluids, how it causes us to be tall or short, and so forth.

But here the beings of the third Hierarchy have only limited power. The ability of plants to grow does not originate from their power alone, for in this respect, these beings of the third Hierarchy—the Angeloi, Archangeloi, and Archai—stand in the service of yet higher beings. What we live through, however, before we descend out of the spiritual world into our physical body, what is connected with our more delicate bodily structure, and all that I have just described, all this is caused by our conscious encounter with these beings of the third Hierarchy. And under this instruction which we can receive from them, in accordance with our preparation in our previous earth life, that is, as a result of the instruction we receive for fashioning our ether body out of the forces of the ether reaches, all this occurs during the last pre-birth period, just before we descend from the superphysical into physical existence.

From the foregoing it is evident that our glance must first fall upon what works into our destiny, into our karma out of our inner constitution. For this aspect of karma, I should like to employ the expressions "comfort and discomfort in life." Well-being, comfort, and discomfort in life are connected with what is our inner quality by virtue of our ether body.

A second element which lives in our karma depends upon the fact that the earth is not only covered by the plant kingdom, but is inhabited by the animal kingdom. Now just consider, my dear friends, that the different regions of the earth have the most varied animals. The animal atmosphere in the different regions of the earth varies greatly.

You will, however, admit that the human being also lives in this atmosphere in which the animals live. That sounds grotesque at the present time, because human beings are not accustomed to consider such matters. There are, for example, regions where the elephant lives. Indeed, in the regions where the elephant lives the cosmos affects the earth in such a way as to make it possible for the elephant to come into being. Indeed, do you believe, my dear friends, that, if there is a portion of the earth upon which the elephant lives, with the elephant-forming forces working down upon it from the cosmos, the same forces are not working, if right at this same spot a human being is present? Of course, these forces are there also when a human being is present. And this is likewise just as true for the whole animal kingdom. In exactly the same way that the plant-forming forces from the ether reaches are present right here where we live—the walls of wood, stone, and even concrete do not hold them back; here in Dornach, we live more or less in the midst of the very forces that fashion the plants in the Jura Alps—so likewise, if a human being lives on the very soil where the elephant can exist according to the earth's constitution, does he live under the elephant-forming forces.

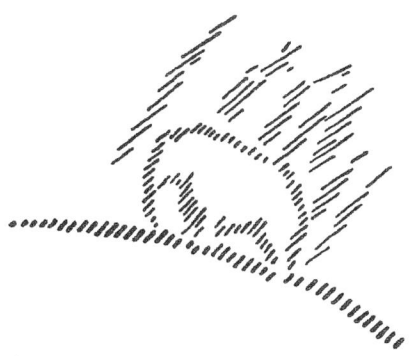

Figure II

I can, indeed, quite well imagine that you now have before your mind's eye many a large and small animal which inhabits the earth, and you now learn that the human being, indeed, lives in the same atmosphere as these animals. All this actually works upon the human being. Naturally, it acts upon the human being differently from the way it acts upon the animals, because the human being has yet other qualities, yet other members of his being than the animals. It acts differently upon the human being; otherwise he would also become an elephant in the elephant sphere. He does not, however, become an elephant. Moreover, the human being lifts himself continually out of what works upon him there. Yet he lives in this atmosphere.

You see, everything that exists in the astral body of the human being is dependent upon this atmosphere in which he lives. And, if we may say that his well-being or discomfort is dependent upon the plant nature of the earth, so may we again say that the sympathies and antipathies which we, as man, develop within our earth existence, and which we bring with us from pre-earthly existence, depend on what constitutes, so to speak, the animal atmosphere.

The elephant has a trunk and thick, column-shaped legs. The stag has antlers, and so on. In these members live the animal-forming, the animal-shaping forces. In the human being these forces are manifest only in their effect upon his astral body. And in this effect upon his astral body they produce the sympathies and antipathies which the human individuality brings with him out of the spiritual world.

Just observe, my dear friends, these sympathies and antipathies. Observe what a strong dominant power these sympathies and antipathies have throughout the whole of life. Certainly, we human beings are taught, with justification in a certain respect, to rise above these strong sympathies and antipathies. Nevertheless, to begin with they still exist—these sympathies and antipathies; we still go through our lives living in sympathies and antipathies. One has sympathy for this and another for that. One has sympathy for sculpture, another for music; one has sympathy for blondes, another for brunettes. These are strong, radical sympathies. But our entire life is interwoven by such sympathies and antipathies. We live in dependence upon those forces which produce the manifold animal configurations.

And now, just ask yourselves, my dear friends, what then do we as human beings bear within us which corresponds within our own innermost being to the manifold animal shapes existing in outer nature? A hundredfold, a thousandfold are the animal shapes. A hundredfold, a thousandfold are the configurations of our sympathies and antipathies; only, most of them remain in the unconscious or in the subconscious.

This is an additional, a third, world.

The first world was the world upon which we really feel no dependence—the mineral world. The second world is the one in which Angeloi, Archangeloi, and Archai live, the one which causes the plant kingdom to sprout forth, which gives us our inner quality by means of which we carry well-being and discomfort into life, by means of which we feel desperately unhappy through ourselves, or feel happy through ourselves. That which signifies our destiny through our inner composition, through our entire etheric humanness, is taken out of this second world. We now come to what further profoundly conditions our destiny,—that is, our sympathies and antipathies. And these sympathies and antipathies bring us, finally, what belongs to our destiny in a far wider scope than do merely these sympathies and antipathies themselves.

The one human being is carried by his sympathies and antipathies into far distances. He lives here and there, because his sympathies have borne him thither, and in these distant reaches the details of his destiny develop. Deeply linked to our whole human destiny are these sympathies and antipathies. They live in the world in which lives not the third Hierarchy, but the second Hierarchy—the Exusiai, the Dynamis, the Kyriotetes. That which is an earthly reflection of the sublime, glorious forms of this second Hierarchy lives in the animal kingdom. That, however, which these beings transplant into us during our intercourse with them between death and a new birth we bring with us out of the spiritual into the physical world as our inborn sympathies and antipathies.

If we fathom these matters, then such concepts as those of ordinary heredity become childish, really childish. For in order that I may possess some inherited trait from my father or mother, I must first develop the sympathy or antipathy for this trait of my father or mother. Thus it does not depend merely upon the fact that I have inherited these qualities through some sort of lifeless nature-cause, but it depends upon whether I have had any sympathy for these qualities. The reason why I have had such sympathies for these qualities will be discussed in the subsequent lectures. Our discussions about karma will, indeed, occupy us for many hours to come. It is, however, really childish to speak about heredity in the way this usually occurs today in those scientific circles which consider themselves especially clever.

It is even asserted today that specifically soul-spirit characteristics are inherited. Genius is said to be inherited from the forebears, and when a genius appears in the world, we seek out the individual traits in the forebears which, when united in some personality, are supposed to produce this genius. Indeed, that is a strange kind of demonstration of the truth. A reasonable proof would be that, if a genius exists he would then, through heredity, again produce another genius. But, if we were to look for these proofs—well, Goethe also had a son, and other geniuses have had sons—we would come upon curious things. That would be a proof! But the fact that a genius exists and that certain characteristics of his forebears are found in this genius has no more significance than that I am wet if I fall into the water and am pulled out. Through this event, I have very little to do in my own nature with the water which then drips from me. Naturally, since I am born into a certain hereditary stream, because of my sympathies with the qualities in question, I am vested with these inherited qualities just as, when I have fallen into the water, I carry some of this water on my body after having been pulled out of it. Grotesquely childish, however, are the ideas which people have in this regard. For the sympathies and antipathies have already appeared in the pre-earthly existence of the human being, and these give him his innermost structure. With these he enters into earth existence: with these he frames his destiny for himself out of his pre-earthly existence.

And we can now easily imagine the following: In a previous earth life, we were associated with a human being. Much has resulted from this association, which continues on in the life between death and a new birth. Under the influence of the forces of the higher Hierarchies, there is fashioned within the living thoughts, within the living cosmic impulses, all that which is then to pass over into the next earth life out of the experience of the previous one, in order to be lived further. For that purpose we employ sympathies and antipathies, cultivating the impulses through which we find each other in life.

And these sympathies and antipathies are shaped under the influence of the Exusiai, Dynamis, Kyriotetes in the life between death and a new birth. These sympathies and antipathies enable us then to find the human beings in life with whom we must continue to live, in accordance with the previous earth lives. This is fashioned out of our inner human structure.

Naturally, in this acquiring of sympathies and antipathies the most manifold errors occur. These, however, are equalized again in the course of destiny throughout many earth lives. Thus we have here a second constituent of karma: the sympathies and antipathies.

We may say: First constituent of karma—inner comfort, or discomfort; second constituent—sympathies and antipathies (see tabulation pages 26, 27). By virtue of our having reached the sympathies and antipathies in human destiny we have ascended into the sphere in which lie the forces for the formation of the animal kingdom.

Now we ascend into the real kingdom of man. We live not only in association with the plant kingdom, with the animal kingdom, but we live quite determinatively for our fate in association with other human beings in the world. That is quite a different association from the association with plants and animals. It is an association through which the chief element of our destiny is fashioned. The impulses which cause the peopling of the earth also with human beings act only upon mankind. And now the question arises: Which are the impulses that act only upon mankind? Here we can permit a purely external consideration to speak which I have already frequently presented.

Our life is, indeed, directed from its yonder side—if I may so express myself—with a much greater wisdom than we direct it here from this side.

We often meet in our later years some one who is extraordinarily important for our life. If we think back and see how we have lived up to the time when we met this human being, our whole life then appears to us to be the path we have taken in order to encounter him. It is as if we had ordered every step so as to find this individual exactly at the right point of time, or at least to find him at a certain point of time.

We need only, for once, ponder upon the following: Just think what, with full human awareness, it signifies, to find in some year of one's life a certain person and henceforward to experience something in common with him, to work and collaborate with him. Just consider what this means. Let us consider in full awareness what it is that offers itself as the impulse which has led us to meet this person. If we ponder upon the matter and ask ourselves how it is that we have found this person, perhaps it will then occur to us that an event had first to be experienced by us which was connected with many other people; otherwise there would not have been the least possibility of finding this human being during life. And in order that this event might occur, another had in turn to be experienced. We arrive at complicated relationships all of which had to take place and into which we had to enter in order to have some decisive experience. And then we ponder, perhaps, upon the following: If at a certain age—I will not say at the age of one, but of fourteen—we had been put to the task of solving consciously the problem how we should, in the fiftieth year of our life, bring about a decisive meeting with some person, if we imagine that at a certain age we should have had to solve this problem consciously like a problem in arithmetic, I beg you just to consider what all of that would require! We human beings are, indeed, consciously extremely stupid, and what happens with us in the world is, if we consider such things, extremely clever and wise!

If we consider such a thing, our attention is directed to the extreme intricacy and significance of our destiny's working, of the action of our karma. And all this occurs in the realm of the human being.

Now, I beg you to consider that what takes place here with us is actually living in the unconscious. Right up to the moment when a critical event confronts us, it lies in the unconscious. Everything takes place as though subject to the laws of nature. But where would the laws of nature ever have the power to effect such a thing? What occurs in this region can, indeed, contradict all nature laws and everything that we construct in accordance with the outer laws of nature. I have repeatedly drawn your attention also to this fact.

The externalities of human life may even be stretched into the frame of calculated laws. Let us take, for example, the business of life insurance. It can only prosper through our being able to calculate the probable life duration of any—let us say—nineteen or twenty year old individual. When some one wishes to insure his life, the policy is based upon the probable length of life. That is, as a person, nineteen years old today, we are expected to live according to these calculations a certain number of years. That can be determined. But just suppose that this period has elapsed. You would not feel in duty bound to die because of this fact. According to this probable life duration, two human beings should have been dead for a long time. But, after they have long been "dead," according to this probable duration of life, they meet each other for the first time in the way I have described! All this occurs beyond what we calculate for human life out of the external facts of nature. And nevertheless it occurs with as much inner necessity as do the laws of nature. It is not possible to say anything but the following: With the same necessity with which any natural phenomenon takes place, an earthquake, or a volcanic eruption, or whatever it may be, a minor or a major event in nature, with the same necessity two human beings meet each other during earth life according to the rules of life which they have made for themselves. Thus we see actually here within the physical realm a new realm established, and within this realm we live not only in comfort or discomfort, in sympathies and antipathies, but we live within it as in our own occurrences, our own experiences. We are entirely moulded into the realm of events, of experiences which determine our life in accordance with destiny.

In this realm the beings of the first Hierarchy are active, the Seraphim, Cherubim, and Thrones. For, in order that every human step, every movement of the soul, everything in us may be guided in the world in such a way that the destiny of man may grow from it, a greater power is needed than that which acts in the plant kingdom, than that possessed by the Hierarchy of the Angeloi, Archangeloi, Archai, than that possessed by the Hierarchy of the Exusiai, Kyriotetes, Dynamis. To achieve this a power is needed which is inherent in the first Hierarchy, Seraphim, Cherubim, Thrones—the most exalted beings of the universe. Now, what comes to manifestation there lives in our real ego, in our ego organism, and extends its life from a previous earth existence into a later one.

    Archai, Archangeloi, Angeloi: First Constituent of Karma
                                                    —Comfort, Discomfort.

Dynamis, Exusiai, Kyriotetes: Second Constituent of Karma—Sympathies, Antipathies.

Seraphim, Cherubim, Thrones: Third Constituent of Karma—Events, Experiences.

And now consider the following: You live a life on earth, causing this or that, out of instincts, passions, inclinations, let us say, or out of clever or foolish thoughts. All this is actually present within you as impulses. Consider that, when you live a life on earth, what you do through instincts leads to this or to that; it leads to the happiness or injury of another human being. Then you pass through the life between death and a new birth. In this life you have the strong consciousness: "If I have injured another human being, I am less perfect than I should have been had I not thus injured him. I must atone for it." You feel in yourself the urge and the impulse to expiate this injury. If you have done something to a human being which advances him, then you behold what is advancing him in such a way that you say: "This must serve as the basis for general world advancement, this must lead to further results in the world."

All this you are able to develop inwardly; all this may give well-being, ease, or discomfort, according to the way you fashion the inner nature of your body during life between death and a new birth. All this may lead you to sympathies and antipathies, in that you construct your astral body in the corresponding way with the help of the beings of the second Hierarchy, the Exusiai, Dynamis, and Kyriotetes. But all of this does not yet give you the power to cause what in a past life were mere human deeds to become a cosmic act. You advanced or injured a human being. The effect of this must be that this human being will encounter you in the next life and that you will find through this encounter the impulse to expiate the effect. What has a merely moral significance must become an outer fact, must become an outer world event.

For this purpose the beings are needed who transform, metamorphose, moral acts into world deeds. These are the beings of the first Hierarchy, Seraphim, Cherubim, and Thrones. These beings transform what proceeds from us in one earth life into our experiences of the next earth lives. They act in what constitutes event and experience in human life.

We have there the three basic elements in our karma; that which composes our inner constitution, our inner human existence, is under the control of the third Hierarchy; that which exists as our sympathies and antipathies, that which in a certain way becomes our environment, is the concern of the second Hierarchy; finally, that which confronts us as our outer life is the concern of the first, the most exalted Hierarchy of beings ranging above men.

Thus we look into the relationship in which the human being stands to the universe, and come now to the important question: How do all the details of our destiny develop from these three elements of the human being?

The human being is born into a parental home. He is born on a certain spot of the earth. He is born within a folk. He is born into a certain complex of facts. Everything, however, that appears by virtue of his being born into a parental home, of his being entrusted to educators, of his being born into a folk, of his being placed upon a certain spot on the earth at his birth,—all of this which, in spite of all human freedom, intervenes so profoundly, so fatefully in the life of the human being, all of this is finally, in some way, dependent upon these three elements which compose human destiny.

All individual questions will disclose themselves to us in corresponding answers, if we focus our attention upon these fundamentals in the right way. If we ask why some one in his twenty-fifth year has small pox, thus passing through the most extreme danger of life, if we ask why some other sickness or event may intervene in his life, why his life may be benefited by this or that older person, by this or that nation, or why advancement occurs to him through this or that outer event,—in every case we shall have to return to that which, in a threefold manner, composes human destiny and places the human being in the totality of the cosmic Hierarchies. In the mineral kingdom alone does the human being move about freely. There lies the realm of his freedom.

By paying attention to this, the human being learns also to pose in the right way the question of freedom. Read in my *Philosophy of Spiritual Activity* how much I have stressed the importance of not asking about the freedom of the will. The will resides deep down in the unconscious, and it is nonsense to ask about the freedom of the will; on the contrary, it is possible to speak only of the freedom of thinking, of thought. In my *Philosophy of Spiritual Activity* I have clearly made this distinction. Free thoughts must activate the will, then is the human being free. But with his thoughts the human being lives in the mineral kingdom. With everything else, with his life in the world of the plant, of the animal, in the purely human world, he is subject to destiny. And freedom is something of which one may say the following: The human being steps out of the realms which are ruled by the higher Hierarchies into the realm which, in a certain way, is independent of the higher Hierarchies, into the mineral kingdom, in order to be free as far as he is concerned. This mineral kingdom is, indeed, the realm to which the human being becomes similar only as a corpse, when he has laid his body aside after having passed through the portal of death. The human being is independent in his earth life of that kingdom which can only act for his destruction. It is not to be wondered at that he is free in this kingdom, since this kingdom has no other part in him but to destroy him when it receives him. He must first die in order that he be, as a corpse, in the realm in which he is free also as a phenomenon of nature. Thus things are related.

We grow older and older. If the other incidents do not occur which we shall also learn about in connection with karma, if the human being dies at an advanced age, he becomes similar, as a corpse, to the mineral kingdom. He enters the sphere of the lifeless by growing older. Then he detaches his corpse from himself. That is no longer human; naturally, it is no longer human. Let us contemplate the mineral kingdom: that is no longer God. Just as the corpse is no longer human, is the mineral kingdom no longer God. What is it, then? The Godhead is in the plant, animal, and human kingdoms; we have found it there in its three Hierarchies. The Godhead is in the mineral kingdom just as little as the human corpse is the human being. The mineral kingdom is the divine corpse. To be sure, we shall encounter in due course the peculiar fact, upon which today I desire only to touch, that the human being grows older in order to become a corpse and the Gods grow younger in order to become a corpse. That is to say, the Gods travel on that other path on which we travel after our death. The mineral kingdom is, therefore, the youngest kingdom. It is, nevertheless, the one that the Gods detach from themselves. And because it is detached from the Gods, the human being can live within it as in the realm of his freedom. Thus are these things interrelated. And the human being learns actually to feel more and more at home in the world by his learning in this way to place his sensations, his thoughts, his feelings, his will impulses in the right relationship to the world. But only thus do we see also how, in accordance with the laws of destiny, we are placed in the world and in relationship to other human beings.

III

Dornach, February 23, 1924

KARMA is best understood by contrasting it with that other impulse in man—the impulse which we indicate by the word *freedom*. Let us first, in a very crude way, I should say, place the question of karma before us. What does it signify?

In human life we have to record the fact of successive earth lives. By feeling ourselves within a given earth life, we can look back—in thought at least, to begin with—and see how this present earth life is a repetition of a number of previous earth lives. It was preceded by another, and that in turn by yet another life on earth, and so on until we get back into the ages where it is impossible to speak of repeated earth lives as we do in the present epoch of the earth, for in going farther backward, we reach a time when the life between birth and death and the life between death and a new birth become so similar that the immense difference which exists between them today is no longer present. Today we live in our earthly body between birth and death in such a way that in every-day consciousness we feel cut off from the spiritual world. Out of this every-day consciousness, men speak of the spiritual world as a "beyond." They even speak of it as though they might doubt its existence, as though they might deny it altogether, and so forth.

This is because man's life within earthly existence restricts him to the outer world of the senses, and to the intellect; the latter does not look far enough to perceive what really is connected with this earthly existence. Out of this, countless arguments arise, all of which actually are rooted in something unknown. No doubt, you will have often stood among people and experienced how they argued about monism, dualism, and so forth. It is, of course, quite absurd to argue about these catch-words. When people argue in this way, we are reminded of some primitive man, let us say, who has never heard that there is such a substance as air. It will not occur to any one who knows that air exists, and what its functions are, to speak of it as something belonging to the beyond. Nor will he think of declaring: "I am a monist; air, water, and earth are one, and you are a dualist, because you regard air as something that extends beyond the earthly and watery elements."

All these things are pure nonsense, as, indeed, are mostly all arguments about concepts. There can, therefore, be no question of our entering into such matters, but it can only be a question of drawing attention to them. For just as the air is not present for the one who knows nothing about it, but for him is something belonging to the "beyond," so for those who do not yet know the spiritual world, which also exists everywhere just as the air, this spiritual world is something belonging to the "beyond;" but for those who take the matter into consideration, the spiritual world is something that belongs very much to this side. Thus it is simply a question of our acknowledging the fact that at the present earth period the human being between birth and death lives in his physical body, in his whole organism, in such a way that this organism gives him a consciousness whereby he is cut off from a certain world of causes which, none the less, affects this physical earth existence.

Then, between death and a new birth he lives in another world, which we may call a spiritual world in contrast to our physical world; in this spiritual world he does not have a physical body which can be made visible to human senses, but he lives in a spiritual nature. And in this life between death and a new birth the world through which he passes between birth and death is just as alien, in turn, as the spirit world is now alien to every-day consciousness.

The dead look down onto the physical world just as the living—that is the physically living—look upward into the spiritual world, and only the feelings are, so to speak, reversed. While the human being here in the physical world between birth and death has a certain aspiration toward another world which grants him fulfilment of much of which there is too little in this world, or of which this world affords him no satisfaction, he must between death and a new birth on account of the multitude of events, and because too much happens in proportion to what a human being can bear, feel a constant longing to return to earth life, to what is then the life in the beyond; hence, during the second half of the life between death and a new birth, he awaits with great longing the passage through birth into a new earth existence. Just as in earth existence the human being is afraid of death, because an uncertainty prevails about what happens thereafter—for in earth life a great uncertainty prevails for ordinary consciousness about what happens after death—so in the life between death and a new birth the condition is just the reverse, there prevails an excessive certainty about earth life. It is a certainty that stuns the human being, that makes him literally faint, so that he is in a state resembling a fainting dream, a state which fills him with the longing to descend again to earth.

These are only a few indications of the great difference prevailing between the earthly life and the life between death and a new birth. If, however, we now go back, let us say, even only as far as the Egyptian period, from the third on up into the first millenium before the founding of Christianity—and, after all, if we go back into this epoch, we go back to those human beings who were none other than ourselves, in a former earth life—indeed, then, at that time during earth existence, life was quite different from our so brutally clear consciousness of the present day. At present human beings have, indeed, a brutally clear consciousness; they are all so clever—I do not at all intend to be ironical—the people of today are, indeed, all very clever. In contrast to this brutally clear consciousness of today, the consciousness of the human being of the ancient Egyptian period was much more dream-like, a consciousness that did not, like ours, strike against outer objects. It passed through the world, as it were, without striking against objects. Instead, it was filled with pictures which, at the same time, revealed something of the spiritual existing in our environment. The spiritual still penetrated into physical earth existence.

Do not ask: How could a man with this more dream-like consciousness, not the brutally clear consciousness of today, have performed the tremendous tasks which were actually achieved, for instance, in the ancient Egyptian or Chaldean epochs? You need merely call to mind the fact that mad people at times, in certain states of mania, possess an immense increase of their physical forces; they begin to carry things which they could not carry when in a completely clear state of consciousness. It was, indeed, a fact that the physical strength of the human beings of that time was correspondingly greater, although they were perhaps of slighter build than men of today. For, as you know, it does not always follow that a stout man is strong and a thin man weak. But they did not spend their earthly life in observing every detail of their physical actions; their physical deeds went parallel with experiences into which the spiritual world still extended.

And again, when the people of that time were in the life between death and a new birth, then far more of this earthly life extended upward into the life beyond—if I may be allowed to use the expression "upward." Nowadays it is exceedingly difficult to communicate with those who are present in the life between death and a new birth, for languages have gradually assumed a form no longer understood by the dead. Our nouns, for instance, soon after death are absolute gaps in the dead's comprehension of the earthly world. They understand nothing but the verbs, i.e. the words of motion, of action. And while we here on earth have our attention constantly drawn by materialistically minded people to the fact that everything should be defined in an orderly manner, and every concept be limited and sharply defined, the dead no longer know anything of definitions; they only know what is in motion, not what has contours and is limited.

But in more ancient times that which lived on earth as speech, that which lived as usage and habit of thought, was still of such a nature that it extended up into the life between death and a new birth, and the dead still heard an echo of this long after their death, and also an echo of what occurred on earth even after their death.

And if we go still farther back into the time following the catastrophe of Atlantis—the eighth and ninth millenium before the Christian era—the difference between the life on earth and the life in the beyond, if I may so describe it, becomes even more insignificant. And then, as we go backward, we gradually reach the ages when the two lives are similar. We can then no longer speak of repeated earth lives.

Thus, repeated earth lives have their limit as we look backward, just as they will have their limit when we look forward into the future. For what begins quite consciously with Anthroposophy—the extension of the spiritual world into the ordinary consciousness of man—will have the consequence that this earth world will extend, in turn, into the world through which we live between death and a new birth; but, in spite of this, our consciousness will not grow dream-like, but clearer and ever clearer. The difference will once again grow less. So that this living in repeated earth lives is limited by outermost boundaries, which then lead into quite another sort of human existence, where it is meaningless to speak of repeated earth lives, because the difference between the earthly and the spiritual life is not so great as it is today.

If we now assume, however, for the long stretch of the present period of the earth age that behind this earth life there lie others—we must not say countless others, for they can even be counted by exact spiritual-scientific research—if we say: behind our present earth life there lie many others, then we have had certain experiences in these previous earth lives which represented certain relationships between human beings. And the effects of these relationships between human beings, which at that time lived themselves out in what we then underwent, extend into this present earth life in the same way as the effects of what we do in this present earth life extend into our next lives on earth. Thus we have to seek in the former earth life the causes of much that now enters into our present life. Then it is easy for the human being to say: "Thus, what I experience now is conditioned, caused. How can I, then, be a free human being?"

Now, this question is, indeed, a rather significant one, if we consider it in this way. For all spiritual observation shows that in this way the subsequent earth life is conditioned by the earlier ones. On the other hand, the consciousness of freedom absolutely exists. And, when you read my *Philosophy of Spiritual Activity*, you will see that we cannot understand the human being at all, if we are not clear about the fact that his whole soul life tends, is directed, is oriented toward freedom, but a freedom which we have to understand correctly.

Now, it is precisely in my *Philosophy of Spiritual Activity* that you will find an idea of freedom which it is very important to grasp correctly. The point is that we have developed freedom, to begin with, in thought. The fountainhead of freedom is in thought. Man has an immediate consciousness of the fact that he is a free being in his thought. You may rejoin: "But there are many people today who doubt the fact of freedom." Yes, but this only proves that the theoretical fanaticism of people today is often stronger than their direct experience in reality. Because he is so crammed full of theoretical concepts the human being no longer believes in his own experiences. Out of his observations of the processes of nature, he arrives at the idea that everything is conditioned by necessity, every effect has a cause, all that exists has its cause; thus, if I conceive a thought, this has also a cause. He does not at once think of repeated earth lives in this connection, but he imagines that what wells forth from human thinking is caused in the same way as that which comes out of a machine.

As a result of this theory of universal causation, as it is called, the human being blinds himself frequently to the fact that he bears very clearly within himself the consciousness of freedom. Freedom is a fact which we experience, as soon as we really reflect upon ourselves.

Now, there are also those who are of the opinion that the nervous system is just a nature system, conjuring thoughts out of itself. According to this, then, the thoughts would—let us say—be necessary results, just like the flame which burns under the influence of a fuel, and there could be no question of freedom.

These people, however, contradict themselves in talking at all. As I have often related here, I had a friend in my youth, who had a fanatical inclination, at a certain period, to think materialistically. Thus he said: "When I walk, for example, then it is the nerves of the brain, infiltrated by certain causes, which bring my walking into effect." This led, at times, to quite a long debate with him. I finally said to him on one occasion: "Now, look here, you always say: 'I walk.' Why do you not say: 'My brain walks'? If you really believe in your theory, you ought never to say: 'I walk, I take hold of things,' but: 'My brain walks, my brain takes hold of things.' Why do you tell a lie?"

These are the theorists, but there are also the practical men. If they observe any nonsense in themselves which they do not wish to stop, they say: "O, I cannot get rid of that; it is just a part of my nature. It is there of its own accord, and I am powerless against it." There are many such people; they refer to the immutable causation of their own nature. But, as a rule, they do not remain consistent. If they happen to be showing off something they rather like about themselves for which they need no excuse, but on the contrary are glad to receive a little flattery, they then abandon the aforesaid view.

The fundamental fact of the free human being—a self-evident fact— can be directly experienced. Now, even in the ordinary, every day earth life it is a fact that we do many things in complete freedom which, nevertheless, are of such a kind that we cannot easily leave them undone. And yet we do not feel our freedom in the least impaired through this fact.

Let us suppose, for a moment, that you now resolve to build yourself a house. It will take about a year to build it. In a year you will live in it. Will you feel that your freedom has been curtailed through the fact that you then have to say to yourself: "The house is now there, and I must move in, I must live in it; it is a case of compulsion"? No, you will surely not feel your freedom impaired through the fact of your having built a house for yourself. You see, therefore, even in ordinary life these two things stand side by side: You have committed yourself to something. It has thereby become a fact in life, a fact with which you have to reckon.

Now think of all that stems from former lives on earth, with which you have to reckon, because it is due to your own deeds—just as the building of the house is caused by you. Seen in this light, you will not feel your freedom impaired through the fact that your present life on earth is determined by former ones.

Perhaps you will say: "Very well. I will build me a house, but I still wish to remain a free man. I will not let myself be compelled. If I do not like it, I shall, in a year, not move into the new house; I shall sell it." All right! We might also have our opinion about such a procedure; we might, perhaps, have the opinion that, if you do this, you are a person who does not know his own mind. Indeed, we might well have this opinion; but let us disregard this. Let us disregard the fact that a man is such a fanatical upholder of freedom that he constantly makes up his mind to do things, and afterwards out of sheer "freedom" leaves them undone. We then might well say: "That man has not even the freedom to enter upon the things he himself resolves upon. He constantly feels the goad of the will to be free, and is positively persecuted by his fanatical worship of freedom."

It is really important that these things not be taken in a rigid, theoretical manner, but be grasped in fullness of life. Let us now pass over to a more complicated concept. If we ascribe freedom to man, surely we must also ascribe it to the higher beings who are not hampered in their freedom by the limitations of human nature. If we rise to the beings of the higher Hierarchies, who certainly are not hampered by the limitations of human nature, we must, indeed, seek a higher degree of freedom with them. Now someone might propose a rather strange theological theory to the effect that God must surely be free; He has arranged the world in a certain way; He has, however, thereby committed Himself; He certainly cannot change the world-order every day; thus, after all, He would in that case be unfree.

You see, if in this way you place in antithesis inner karmic necessity and freedom, which is a fact of our consciousness, which is simply a result of self-observation, you cannot then escape a continuous circle. In this way you cannot escape from a circle. For the matter is as follows: Let us take once more the illustration of the building of a house. I do not wish to press this example too far, but at this point it can still help us along the way. Some one builds himself a house. I will not say: *I* build myself a house—I shall probably never build one for myself—but, let us say, some one builds himself a house. Well, by this resolve he does, in a certain respect, determine his future. Now, when the house is finished, and he takes his former resolve into account, no freedom apparently remains for him, so far as the living in the house is concerned. He himself has certainly set this limitation to his freedom; nevertheless, apparently no freedom remains for him.

But just think, how many things still remain for you to do in freedom within this house. Indeed, within it you are even free to be stupid or wise, you are free to be horrid or lovable to your fellow men. In the house you are free to get up early or late. Perhaps, you may be under other obligations in this respect; but so far as the house is concerned, you are free to get up early or late. You are free to be an anthroposophist or a materialist within this house. In short, there are innumerable things still at your free disposal.

Likewise in an individual human life, in spite of the presence of karmic necessity, there are countless things at your free disposal, far more than in a house, countless things fully and really in the domain of freedom.

Here you may, perhaps, be able to rejoin: "Very well, we do then have a certain domain of freedom in our life." Indeed, that is so: a certain enclosed domain of freedom surrounded by the karmic necessity (see Figure III). Now, looking at this, you may assert the following. You may say: "Well, I am free in a certain domain; but I now reach the limits of my freedom. I then feel the karmic necessity everywhere. I walk around in my room of freedom, but everywhere at the boundaries I come up against my karmic necessity and sense this necessity."

Figure III

Indeed, my dear friends, if a fish thought likewise, it would be extremely unhappy in the water, for as it swims in the water it reaches the water's boundary. Outside of the water it can no longer live. Hence it refrains from going outside of the water. It does not go at all outside of the water; it remains in the water, it swims around in the water, and it just lets alone the other element which lies beyond, be it air or something else. And because the fish does this, I can assure you that it is not at all unhappy over the fact that it cannot breathe with lungs. It does not occur to it to be unhappy. But, if ever it did occur to the fish to be unhappy because it breathes only with gills and not with lungs, then it would have to have lungs in reserve, then it would have to compare the difference between living down below in the water, and up in the air. Then the fish's whole way of feeling itself inwardly would be different. It would all be quite different.

If we apply this comparison to human life with respect to freedom and karmic necessity, then it is a fact, in the first place, that the human being in the present earth period has the ordinary consciousness. With this ordinary consciousness he lives in the sphere of freedom, just as the fish lives in the water, and with this consciousness he does not enter at all the realm of karmic necessity. Only when he begins really to perceive the spiritual world—this would be similar to the fish having lungs in reserve—only when he really finds his way into the spiritual world, does he acquire a perception of the impulses living in him as karmic necessity. He then looks back into his former lives on earth and does not feel, does not say, on finding the causes of his present experiences in a previous earth life: "I am now under the compulsion of an iron necessity, and my freedom is impaired," but he looks back and sees how he himself has fashioned what now confronts him, just as some one who has built himself a house looks back on the resolve which led him to build it. And we generally find it more reasonable to ask: "Was it, at that time, a sensible or foolish resolve to build this house?" Well, naturally, we can come later on to all sorts of opinions on the matter, if the things turn out in a certain way; but, if we find that it was an enormous stupidity to build the house, we can, at best, say that we were foolish.

Now, in earth life it is an awkward matter in regard to anything which one has inaugurated to have to say that it was stupid. We do not like this. We do not like to suffer from our own follies. We wish we had not made the foolish decision. But this really applies only to the one earth life, because between the foolishness of the resolve and the punishment we suffer in having to experience its consequences there lies the same earth life. It always remains thus.

But this is not so between the individual earth lives. For between them always lie the lives between death and a new birth; and these lives between death and a new birth change many things which would not change if earth life were to continue uniformly. Just suppose that you look back into a former earth life. There you did something good or ill to another human being. The life between death and a new birth took place between this previous earth life and the present earth life. In this life, in this spiritual life, you cannot think otherwise than that you have become imperfect by having done something evil to another human being. This takes away from your value as a human being. It cripples you in soul. You must repair the crippling, and you resolve to achieve in a new earth life what will make good the fault. Thus, between death and a new birth you absorb by your own will that which will compensate for the fault. If you have done good to another human being, you then know that the whole of human life is there for the whole of mankind. You see this most clearly in the life between death and a new birth. You then realize that when you have helped another human being, he has thereby achieved certain things which, without you, he would not have achieved in a former earth life; but, as a result, you feel again united with him in the life between death and a new birth, in order now to live and to develop further what you have achieved together with him in regard to human perfection. You seek him out again in a new earth life in order, in this new earth life, to work further with him through the way you have already helped him perfect himself.

The fact is not at all that we might abhor such necessity, when we, through a real insight into the spirit world, now perceive the scope of this karmic necessity all around us, but the fact is that we look back upon this necessity and see how the things were which we ourselves had done, and then behold them in such a way that we say: "What occurs out of inner necessity *has to happen*—out of complete freedom also it *would have to happen.*"

We shall never have the experience of possessing a real insight into karma without being in agreement with it. If things result in the course of karma which do not please us, then we ought to consider them from the point of view of the general laws and principles of the universe. And we shall then realize more and more that, after all, what is karmically conditioned is better than our having to begin anew, better than our being a book of blank pages with every new earth life. For, as a matter of fact, we are ourselves our karma. We are ourselves that which comes over from previous earth lives. And it has no sense at all to say that something in our karma—alongside of which there exists definitely the realm of freedom—that something in our karma ought to be different from what it is, because it is not at all possible to criticize the single detail in an organically connected totality. Some one may not like his nose; but it is senseless to criticize merely the nose, as such, for the nose a man has must actually be as it is, if the whole man is as he is. The one who says: "I should like to have a different nose," actually says that he would like to be an utterly different man. But in so doing he really eliminates himself in thought. This we cannot do. Thus we cannot wipe out our karma, for we are ourselves our karma. Nor does it at all confound us, for it runs its course alongside the deeds of our freedom, and in no wise interferes with the deeds of our freedom.

I should like to use still another comparison to make the point clear. As human beings, we walk; but the ground on which we walk is also there. No one feels interfered with in walking by having the ground underneath his feet. Indeed, he ought even to know that, were the ground not there, he could not walk at all; he would fall through everywhere. It is thus with our freedom; it needs the "ground" of necessity. It must rise out of a foundation. And this foundation—we ourselves are.

As soon as we grasp in the right way the concept of freedom and the concept of karma, we shall be able to find them compatible, and we then need no longer shrink from a detailed study of the karmic laws. Indeed, in some instances we may even come to the following conclusion:

I now assume that some one, by means of the insight of initiation, is able to look back into former earth lives. He knows quite well, when he looks back into former earth lives that this and that has happened to him which has come with him into his present earth life. Had he not attained to initiation science, objective necessity would impel him to do certain things. He would do them quite inevitably. He would not feel his freedom hampered by it; for his freedom lies in his ordinary consciousness with which he never penetrates into the realm where this necessity acts, just as the fish never penetrates into the outer air. But when he has initiation science within him, he then looks back and he sees how things were in a former earth life, and he regards what now confronts him as a task which is consciously allotted to him for this present earth life. This is, indeed, a fact.

What I shall now say may sound paradoxical to you, yet it is true. In reality, a man who possesses no initiation science practically always knows through a kind of inner urge, through an instinct, what he is to do. O, indeed, people always know what they ought to do, feel themselves always impelled to this thing or that. For the one who begins with initiation science, matters become somewhat different in the world. As he faces life, quite strange questions arise in regard to the individual experiences. If he feels impelled to do something, he immediately feels also impelled not to do it. The obscure urge which drives most human beings to this or that is eliminated. And, actually, at a certain stage of initiate-insight, if nothing else were to intervene, a man could really come to the point of saying to himself: "After having reached this insight, I now prefer to spend the entire remainder of my life—I am now 40 years old, which is a matter of indifference to me—sitting on a chair doing nothing. For such pronounced urges to do this or that are no longer present."

Do not believe, my dear friends, that initiation does not have a reality. It is strange, in this connection, how people sometimes think. In regard to a roast chicken, everyone who eats it believes that it has reality. In regard to initiate science, most people believe that it has only theoretical effects. No, it has effects on life. And such a life effect is the one I have just indicated. Before a man has attained to initiation, under the influence of an obscure urge, one thing is always important to him and another unimportant. The initiate would prefer to sit in a chair and let the world run its course, for it really does not matter—so it might appear to him— whether this is done and that is left undone, and so forth. It will, however, not remain so, for initiation science also offers something else besides. The only corrective for the initiate's sitting on a chair, letting the world run its course, and saying: "everything is a matter of indifference to me," is to look back into former earth lives. He then reads there from his karma the tasks for his present earth life, and he does consciously what his former earth lives impose upon him. He does not abstain from doing it because he believes that thereby his freedom is encroached on, but he does it. He does it, because by his discovery of what he had experienced in previous earth lives he becomes aware, at the same time, of what his life between death and a new birth has been, how he then realized the performance of the corresponding consequential actions as something reasonable. He would feel himself unfree if he could not come into the position of fulfilling the task which is allotted to him by his former earth life.

Thus, neither before nor after the entry into initiation science is there a contradiction between karmic necessity and freedom. Before the entry into initiation science, there is none, because with every-day consciousness the human being remains within the realm of freedom, while karmic necessity takes place outside, like a process of nature. He has nothing that feels different from what his own nature inspires in him. Nor is there any contradiction after the entry into initiation science, because he is then quite in agreement with his karma and simply considers it reasonable to act in harmony with karma. Just as you do not say, if you have built yourself a house: "the fact that I must now move in is hampering my freedom," but just as you will probably say: "well, on the whole it was quite sensible to build myself a house in this neighborhood and on this site; now, let me be free in this house!" so likewise the one who looks back with initiate knowledge into former earth lives knows that he becomes free by fulfilling his karmic task, by moving into the house which he built for himself in former earth lives.

Thus, my dear friends, I wanted to explain to you the true compatibility of freedom and karmic necessity in human life. Tomorrow we shall continue, going more into the details of karma.

IV

Dornach, February 24, 1924

TODAY I wish, primarily, to bring before you some of the more comprehensive aspects in the development of karma, in order to be able gradually to go more and more into matters of detail. If we wish to gain insight into the course of karma, we must be able to imagine how the human being gathers his whole organization together as he descends out of the spiritual world into the physical. You will understand, my dear friends, that in the language of today there are no suitable expressions for certain processes which are practically unknown to modern civilization, and that, therefore, the expressions employed here for what takes place under certain conditions can only be approximate.

When we descend out of the spiritual into the physical world for an earth life, we have, to begin with, prepared our physical body by means of the stream of heredity. We shall see how this physical body is, nevertheless, connected in a certain sense with what the human being experiences between death and a new birth. Today, however, it will suffice if we are clear about the fact that the physical body is given to us from the earth; on the other hand, those members which we may describe as the higher members of the human being—the ether body, astral body, and ego—come down from the spiritual world.

The human being attracts, so to speak, the ether body out of the whole universal ether before he unites himself with the physical body which is given to him by heredity. The union of the soul-spirit man—i.e. ego, astral body, and ether body—with the physical human embryo can ensue only through the gradual withdrawal of the ether body of the maternal organism from the physical human embryo.

The human being, thus, unites himself with the physical germ after having attracted his ether body out of the common universal ether. The more precise descriptions of these events will occupy us later. At present we are to interest ourselves mainly in asking: Whence come the individual members of human nature which the human being possesses during earth life between birth and death?

The physical organism comes, as we have seen, from the stream of heredity, the etheric organism out of the universal ether from which it is attracted. The astral organism—of which the human being remains, we might say, in all respects unconscious or only sub-consciously aware during his earth life—this astral body contains all the results of the life between death and a new birth. And it is a fact that between death and a new birth, according to what the human being has become through his preceding earth lives, he comes, in the most manifold way, into relationship with other human souls who are also in the life between death and a new birth, or with other spiritual beings of a higher cosmic order who do not descend to earth in a human body, but have their existence in the spiritual world.

All that a man brings over from his former lives on earth according to what he was, according to what he has done, all this is met by the sympathy or antipathy of the beings whom he learns to know while he passes through the world between death and a new birth. What sympathies and antipathies he meets among the higher beings according to what he has done in his preceding earth life is of great significance for karma during this period; but, above all, it is of deep significance that he comes into relationship with those human souls with whom he was in relationship on earth, and that a peculiar reflection takes place between his own nature and the nature of the souls with whom he had this relationship. Let us assume that some one has had a good relationship with a soul whom he now encounters again between death and a new birth. All that the good relationship implies had lived in him during former earth lives. Then this good relationship is reflected in the soul, when this soul is encountered between death and a new birth. And it is really true that the human being during this passage through the life between death and a new birth sees himself reflected everywhere in the souls with whom he is now associated because he was associated with them on earth. If he did good to a human being, something is mirrored to him from the other soul; if he did him an evil turn, something is likewise mirrored to him from the other soul. And he has the feeling—if I may use the word "feeling" with the reservation made at the beginning of these observations—he has the feeling: "You have advanced this human soul. What you have experienced through advancing him, what you then felt for this soul, that impulse in your feelings which led to your attitude toward him, your own inner experiences in performing the deed that advanced this soul, come back to you from him. They are reflected to you from this soul. In another case you have injured a soul; what has lived in you during this injury is reflected to you."

And the human being has actually spread out before him, as though in a mighty and wide-extending reflector, his previous earth lives, but chiefly the last one, mirrored from the souls with whom he was associated. And we gain the impression, just in regard to our life of action, that all that is departing from us. We lose the ego-feeling which we had on earth in the body, or we really lost it a long time ago between death and a new birth. Now, however, the ego-feeling arises in us from this whole reflection. With the mirroring of our deeds, we come to life in all the souls with whom we were associated during our earth life.

On earth, our I, our ego, was like a point. Here between death and a new birth, it is reflected to us everywhere from the periphery. This is an intimate association with other souls, but an association in accordance with the relations into which we have entered with them.

And in the spiritual world all this is a reality. If we go through a room hung with many mirrors, we see ourselves reflected in each one. But we also know that the reflections—according to ordinary human parlance—are "not there;" when we depart they do not remain; we are no longer reflected. But that which is reflected there in human souls remains as something present. And there comes a time in the last third of the life between death and a new birth when we form our astral body out of these mirrored images. We draw all this together to form our astral body, so that, in truth, when we descend from the spiritual world into the physical, we carry in our astral body what we have taken up again into ourselves, in accordance with the reflection to which our actions of the former earth life have given rise in other souls between death and a new birth. This gives us the impulses which impel us toward or away from the human souls with whom we are born again at the same time in the physical body.

In this way, between death and a new birth, the impulse for the karma of the new earth life is fashioned. I shall, very soon, have to describe the process more in detail by taking the ego into consideration also.

And now we can trace how an impulse from one life works on into other lives. Let us take, for example, the impulse of love. We can perform our deeds in relation to other human beings out of that impulse which we call love. There is a difference whether we perform our acts out of a mere sense of duty, of convention, of decency, or the like, or whether we perform them out of a greater or lesser degree of love.

Let us assume that during an earth life a human being is able to perform actions warmed through and through by love. This, indeed, remains as a real force in his soul. What he now takes with him as result of his deeds, what is mirrored there in the other souls, comes back to him as a reflection. And from this he forms his astral body with which he descends to the earth. There the love of the former earth life, the love which has streamed out of him and which now returns to him from other human beings, transforms itself into joy. So that, when the human being does something for his fellow-men that is sustained by love, something in connection with which love streams out of him and accompanies the deeds which advance his fellow-men, then the metamorphosis in the passage through life between death and a new birth is of such a character that what is outpouring love in one life on earth is, in the next earth life, transmuted, metamorphosed, into joy streaming toward him.

If you experience joy, my dear friends, through a human being in one earth life, you may be sure it is the outcome of the love which you have shown for him in a former life. This joy now flows back again into your soul during earth life. You know this inwardly warming feeling of joy. You know what meaning joy has in life, especially the joy which comes from human beings. It warms life, it sustains life, we may say that it gives wings to life. It is karmically the result of love bestowed.

In our joy, however, we again experience a relation to the other human being who gives us joy. So that in our former earth lives we have had something within us that made the love flow out from us; in our subsequent earth lives we already have, as a result, the inward experience of the warmth of joy. And that is again something that streams from us. A human being who is allowed to experience joy in life, is of importance to his fellow-men, has warming significance. A human being who has cause for going joylessly through life behaves differently toward his fellow-men from the one who is permitted to go through life joyfully.

But what is experienced in joy in the life between birth and death is reflected again in the souls of the most various kinds with whom we were associated on earth and who are now also in the life between death and a new birth. And this reflection, which in manifold ways then comes back to us from the souls of the human beings known to us on earth, this reflection works back in turn. We carry it again in our astral body when we descend into the next earth life—we are now dealing with the third earth life. Once more it is instilled, imprinted, in our astral body. And it now becomes in its result the underlying basis, the impulse for a quick and ready understanding of human beings and the world. It becomes the basis for that soul condition which sustains us by virtue of our having the ability to understand the world. If we find the conduct of human beings interesting and can take joy in it, if we understand their conduct and take interest in it in a given incarnation on earth, then that directs us back to the joy of our previous incarnation, to the love of our still earlier incarnation. Human beings who are able to go through the world with a free and open mind, so that the free and open mind permits the world to flow into them, so that they have an understanding for the world, these are human beings who have gained this attitude to the world through love and joy.

What we perform in our deeds out of love is altogether different from what we do out of a rigid and dry sense of duty. You know, indeed, that I have always emphasized in my books that the deeds springing from love are to be understood as the truly ethical, as the truly moral deeds. I have often been compelled to indicate the great contrast, in this regard, between Kant and Schiller. Kant, both in life and in knowledge, "kantified"* everything. Through Kant, everything in knowledge became sharp and angular; and thus also human conduct. "Duty, thou great and exalted name, thou who containest nothing of pleasure, nothing that curries favors . . .," this passage I quoted in my *Philosophy of Spiritual Activity* to the pretended vexation—not the sincere, but the pretended, hypocritical vexation—of many opponents, and I opposed to it what I must acknowledge to be my view: "Love, thou impulse that speaketh warmly to the soul. . . ."

Over against the dry and rigid Kantian concept of duty, Schiller coined the expression: "Gladly I serve my friends; yet alas, I do it with pleasure, wherefore it oftentimes vexes me that I am not virtuous." For, according to the Kantian ethics, that which we do out of inclination is not virtuous, but only that which we do out of the rigid concept of duty.

Now, there are human beings who, in the first place, do not attain to love. But, because they cannot tell their fellow-man the truth out of love (for if we love a human being we tell him the truth, and not lies), because they are unable to love, they tell the truth out of a sense of duty; since they cannot love, they refrain, merely out of a sense of duty, from thrashing their fellow-man, or boxing his ears, striking him, or doing something similar, when he does anything they do not like. There is, indeed, a

* *Kante* in German means a hard edge or angle. (Note by translator)

difference between the deeds of love and acting out of a rigid sense of duty—which, to be sure, is absolutely necessary in social life, necessary for many things.

Now, the deeds that are done out of a rigid concept of duty, or out of convention or propriety, because it is "the proper thing to do," will not call forth joy in the next earth life, but in that they pass in the same way through the reflection by the souls, as I have described it, they call forth in the next earth life something which we might describe as follows: We sense that we are an object of indifference to other human beings. Many a person carries through life the sense that he is an object of indifference to other human beings, and suffers from it. And rightly he suffers from it, if he is of no concern to other human beings, for human beings are there for one another, and the human being is dependent upon not being a matter of indifference to his fellow-men. What the human being thus suffers here is simply the result of the lack of love in a former earth life where he behaved as a decent human being because of the rigid duty which hung over him like the sword of Damocles—I will not say, a sword of steel, for that would be disquieting for most dutiful people, but just like a wooden sword of Damocles.

We have now reached the second earth life. That which comes as joy from love becomes in the third life, as we have seen, a free and open heart, bringing the world near to us, giving us open-minded insight into all things beautiful and true and good. That which streams to us as indifference from other human beings, and what we experience thereby in one earth life, fashions us for the third, that is to say for the next earth life, into a human being who does not know what to do with himself. When such a person enters school, he is at a loss what to do with that which the teachers impart to him. When he grows a little older, he does not know whether to become a locksmith or Privy Councillor. He does not know what to do with himself in life. He actually drifts aimlessly through life without direction. In regard to his observation of the outer world, he is not exactly dull. Music, for instance, he understands well enough, but it gives him no pleasure. It is, after all, a matter of indifference to him whether the music is more or less good or more or less bad. To be sure, he feels the beauty of a painting or other work of art, but there is always something in his soul that irritates him: "What is the good of it, anyhow? To what purpose is all this?" These, in turn, are the things that make their appearance in karmic connection in the third earth life.

Now let us assume, however, that out of hate or an inclination to antipathy a human being does certain injuries to his fellow-men. Here we may imagine every conceivable degree. One individual with criminal feelings of hatred may harm his fellow-men. Or—I am omitting the intermediate stages—he may be a critic. To be a critic, one must always hate a little—unless one is a praising critic, and such critics are few nowadays, for it is not interesting to show recognition of other people's work; it becomes interesting only when one can make fun of things. Now, there are all manner of intermediate stages. But we have here to think of human deeds which proceed from a cold antipathy—antipathy about which we are often not at all clear—or, at the other extreme, from hatred. All that is brought about in this way by human beings against their fellow-men or even against sub-human creatures, all this vents itself in soul conditions which in turn also mirror themselves in the life between death and a new birth. And then, in the next earth life, out of the hatred is born that which streams to us from the world as sorrow, as unhappiness caused from without, as the opposite of joy.

You will reply: "But really, we experience so much sorrow; is that all due to hatred, greater or lesser hatred, in our preceding life? I cannot possibly imagine"—a man will be apt to say—"that I have been such a bad lot, so that I must experience so much sorrow, because I have hated so much." Well, if we wish to think without prejudice on these things, we must become aware of how great is the illusion which gives us satisfaction and to which, therefore, we easily surrender if it is a question of our suggesting away from our conscious mind any feeling of antipathy against other human beings. People really go through the world with far more hatred than they think—at least, with far more antipathy. And it is a matter of fact that hatred, because it gives satisfaction to the soul, is not as a rule consciously experienced. It is eclipsed by the satisfaction it gives. But, when it returns as sorrow which streams to us from without, then we notice it, as sorrow.

But just consider for a moment, my dear friends—in order to represent in a quite trivial fashion what is present there as a possibility—think of an afternoon-tea chatter, a real, a genuine gossipping tea party where half a dozen (half a dozen is quite enough) "aunts" or "uncles"—it can be uncles, too—or "cousins," if you will, are sitting together discussing their fellows. Just think how many antipathies are unloaded on human beings, say, in the course of an hour and a half—often it is longer. While this antipathy pours out, people do not notice it; but when it returns in the next earth life, then it will, indeed, be noticed. And it returns, inexorably.

Thus, in actual fact, a portion—not all; we shall still become acquainted with other karmic connections—a portion of what we experience in one earth life as sorrow caused from outside may very well be due to our feelings of antipathy in a former earth life.

In connection with all this we must, naturally, always realize that karma, that some sort of karmic stream, must begin at some time, somewhere. So that, if you have here, for example, a succession of earth lives:

$$\underline{a\ b\ c\ (d)}$$

and this (d) is the present life; not all pain, naturally, that falls to our lot from without need be due to our former earth lives. It may also be an original sorrow, which will work itself out karmically only in the next earth life. I say, therefore, that a *large part* of that sorrow which streams to us from outside is a result of hate which was brought into being in former earth lives.

If we now proceed again to the third earth life, the result of what streams to us there as sorrow—but only the result of that sorrow which comes to us, so to speak, out of stored-up hate—the result of this sorrow which then unloads in our soul is, in the first place, a kind of mental dullness, a sort of dullness in the capacity of insight into the world. If you have a human being who confronts the world phlegmatically and with indifference, who does not confront the things of the world, or other human beings, with an open heart, the fact is, very often, that he has acquired this obtuseness of mind through the sorrow of a previous earth life, caused in his own karma. This sorrow, however, when it expresses itself in this way in obtuseness of soul must be retraced to the feelings of hatred which occurred at least in the second earth life prior to this one. We can be absolutely sure that stupidity in any one earth life is always the consequence of hatred in a certain former earth life.

Yet, my dear friends, the understanding of karma shall not rest only on the fact that we comprehend karma for the purpose of understanding life, but that we are also able to comprehend it as an impulse of life, that we are conscious that with life there is not merely an "a, b, c, d," but also an "e, f, g, h,"

$$\underline{a,\ b,\ c,\ (d),\ e,\ f,\ g,\ h}$$

that there are also earth lives still to come, and that what we develop as the content of our soul in a present earth life will have its effects, its results, in the next earth life. If any one wishes to be especially stupid in his second earth life after this one, he need, really, only hate a great deal in this present earth life. But, if some one wishes to have a free and open insight in the second earth life after this one, he need only love with special intensity in this earth life. And insight into karma, knowledge of karma, gains real value only through the fact that it flows into our will for the future, that it plays a role in this will for the future. And it is true in every respect that the moment is now at hand in the evolution of mankind when the unconscious can no longer continue to be effective in the same way it was effective previously, while our souls were passing through previous earth lives, for human beings are becoming constantly freer and more conscious.

Since the first third of the fifteenth century we have been in the age in which human beings are continually becoming freer and more conscious. Hence, those individuals who are human beings of the present time will have in a subsequent earth life a dim feeling of previous earth lives. And just as the modern man, if he notices that he is not very bright, does not ascribe this to himself, but to his natural lack of ability—the cause of which he usually seeks in his physical nature in accordance with the theories of modern materialism—so will the human beings who will be the re-incarnated human beings of the present time, have at least an obscure feeling which will worry them. If they are not very bright, they will feel that something must have taken place which was connected with feelings of hate and antipathy.

And, if we speak today of a Waldorf School pedagogy, we must naturally take into account the present earth civilization. We cannot yet educate in complete frankness in such a way that we consciously employ repeated earth lives in education, for modern human beings have not yet even a dim feeling for repeated earth lives. The beginnings, however, that have been made just in the Waldorf School pedagogy, if they are taken up, will continue to develop in the coming centuries with the result that the following will be included in ethical, moral education: If a child has little talent, it is due to former earth lives in which it has hated intensely, and we shall then, with the help of spiritual science, seek out whom it might have hated. For the human beings who were hated, and against whom deeds were committed out of hate, must be rediscovered somewhere in the child's environment. Gradually, in coming centuries, the education of a child will have to be related far more definitely to human life. We shall have to see, in regard to this dull child, whence that is reflected or has been reflected in the life between death and a new birth, which goes through a metamorphosis resulting in unintelligence in this earth life. We shall then be able to do something to the end that in childhood a special love is developed for those human beings for whom the child felt specific hatred in former earth lives. And we shall see that through such a specifically aroused and directed love, the child's intellect, nay, the child's whole soul state, will brighten.

It is not in general theories about karma that we shall find what can aid education, but in looking concretely into life in order to see what the karmic connections are. We shall soon notice that the fact that children are brought together in a school class by fate is, indeed, not something to be regarded with complete indifference. And when we shall have risen beyond the hideous carelessness that prevails in these things nowadays, when the "human material"—for so it is often called—which is thrown together in a school class is actually conceived as though it were thrown together by mere chance, not as though destiny had brought these human beings together,—if we shall have risen beyond this appalling indifference, we shall then gain a new outlook as educators, we shall then be able to perceive what strange karmic threads are spun from one child to the other as a result of former lives. And we shall then bring into the children's development that which can effect equalization.

In a certain respect, karma is under the domination of an inexorable necessity. Out of an inexorable necessity we are able definitely to establish the sequence:

Love   — Joy   — Open Heart
Antipathy or Hatred — Sorrow — Stupidity

These are unconditional connections. Although it is true that we are confronted by an absolute necessity when a river follows its course, yet we have frequently regulated rivers, have given them a different course. So in like manner is it also possible to regulate, if I may say so, the karmic stream, to affect its course. Indeed, this is possible.

Thus, if you notice that in childhood there is a tendency to idiocy, and if you then realize the necessity of guiding the child, especially of developing love in his heart, if you discover—and this should be possible even today for people with a fine observation of life,—if you discover to which other children the child is karmically related, and if you are able

Figure IV

to bring the child to the point of loving just these children, to perform deeds of love for them, you will then see that you are able with love to give a counterweight to antipathy, and that you are able by means of it to correct this idiocy in the next incarnation, in the next earth life.

There are educators, trained, as it were, by their own instinct, who often do some such thing out of their instinct, who bring dull-witted children to the point where they are able to love, and thus educate them by degrees to become more intelligent human beings.

It is such things that make our insight into karmic connections of service to life.

<pre>
Love   — Joy   — Open Heart
Antipathy — Sorrow — Stupidity
                    Love
</pre>

Before we go further in considering the details of karma, yet another question will have to confront our souls. Just ask yourself: What is a human being really with whom—in general, at least—we may know ourselves to be karmically related? I must use an expression which is often used today rather ironically: such a man is a "contemporary"; he is on the earth at the same time that we are.

If you bear this in mind, you will say to yourself that, if you are associated with certain human beings in one earth life, you were associated with them in a previous earth life also (generally speaking, at least; matters may, of course, be somewhat shifted). And you were, likewise, associated with them in a still earlier life. (See Fig. V)

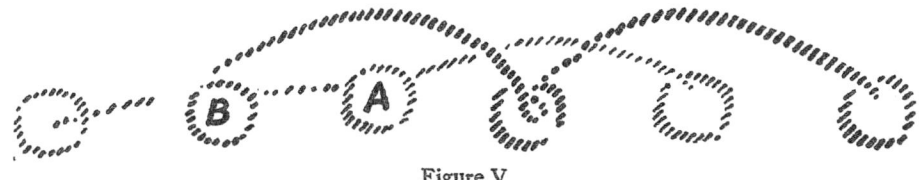

Figure V

Now, those individuals, who live fifty years later than you, were associated in turn with human beings in former earth lives. Generally speaking, the human beings of, let us say, the B series do not, in accordance with the thought we have developed here, come in contact with the human beings of the A series. This is an oppressive thought, but a true one.

I shall later speak about other debatable questions, such as arise, for instance, through the fact that people often say that humanity multiplies on the earth. Today, however, I should like to place the following thought before you; it is, perhaps, an oppressive thought, but it is none the less a true one. It is an actual fact that the continued life of men on earth takes place in rhythms. One shift of human beings—if I may put it so—proceeds, as a general rule, from one earth life to another; another shift of human beings does the same, and they are in a certain sense separated from one another; they do not come together during earth life. To be sure, in the long intervening life between death and a new birth they do come together; but for earth life it is, indeed, a fact that we descend to the earth with a limited circle of people. To be "contemporaries" has an inner meaning, an inner importance just for repeated earth lives.

Why is it so? I can assure you, this question which, in the first place, may occupy us intellectually, has caused me the greatest imaginable pain in the field of spiritual science, because it is necessary to discover the truth regarding this question, the inner nature of the facts. And thus we may ask ourself—forgive my using an example which really concerns me only as a matter of research—we may ask ourself the question: "Why were you not a contemporary of Goethe's? By your not being a contemporary of Goethe's you can, according to this truth, conclude on general principles that you have never lived with Goethe on the earth. Goethe belongs to another shift of human beings."

What really lies behind this? Here we must reverse the question. But to do so we must have an open, liberal mind for human social relationships. We must be able to ask ourself a question—and I shall have very much to say in the near future about this question—we must be able to ask ourself the question: What is it really to be another man's contemporary? What is it, on the other hand, to be able to know of him only from history, so far as the earth life is concerned? What does this mean?

Well, my dear friends, we must have an open, liberal mind in order to answer the intimate question: "How do matters stand with regard to all the inner accompanying phenomena of the soul when a contemporary of yours speaks to you, performs actions which come near you? How do matters stand?" And, after having acquired the necessary knowledge, you must then be able to compare this with what the situation would be were you to come into contact with a personality who is not your contemporary, perhaps has never been such in any life on earth, and whom you may, nevertheless, revere to the highest degree, much more, perhaps, than any of your contemporaries—what would be the situation were you to encounter this personality as a contemporary? In a word—pardon the personal note—what would the situation be, had I been a contemporary of Goethe? If you are not an indifferent kind of person—naturally, if you *are* an indifferent person and have no comprehension of what a contemporary can be, you cannot very well answer such a question—then you can ask the question: "How would it be if I, walking down the Schillergasse in Weimar toward the Frauenplan, had seen the fat Privy Councillor approaching me, say in the year 1826, 1827?" Now, we know quite well, we could not have stood it. Our contemporary we can stand. If the one with whom we cannot be contemporary were, nevertheless, our contemporary, we should not be able to endure him; he would, in a certain sense, act like a poison on our soul life. We endure him as a historical character, because he is not our contemporary, but our successor or predecessor.

Of course, if we have no feeling for such things, they remain in the unconscious. We can well imagine that a certain man has a fine feeling for the spiritual and knows that, had he walked down the Schillergasse in Weimar toward the Frauenplan, and had he, as a contemporary, encountered the fat Privy Councillor Goethe with the double chin, he would then have felt himself in an inwardly impossible state. The one, however, who has no feeling for such things—well, he would, perhaps, have taken off his hat!

These things, my dear friends, do not derive from the earth life, because the reasons why we cannot be the contemporary of some particular man are not to be found within earth life, because here we must penetrate with our preception into the spiritual relationships. This is why, for earth life, such things appear at times paradoxical. Nevertheless, they are facts, most certainly facts.

I can assure you that I wrote with genuine love an Introduction to Jean Paul's works, published in the *Cotta'sche Bibliothek der Weltliteratur*. Yet, if I had ever had to sit side by side with Jean Paul at Bayreuth—without doubt, I should have had a stomach ache. That does not hinder us from having the highest reverence. But such an experience comes to every human being, only, with most people it remains in the subconscious, in the astral or in the ether body; it does not take hold of the physical body. For the soul experience which must seize upon the physical body must, indeed, become conscious. But the following must also be clear to you, my dear friends: If you wish to gain knowledge of the spiritual world, you cannot escape hearing things which seem grotesque and paradoxical, because the spiritual world is different from the physical.

It is, of course, easy enough for any one to ridicule the statement that if I had been a contemporary of Jean Paul's, it would have given me a stomach ache to sit in his company. It goes without saying that for the everyday, banal, phillistine world of earthly life ridicule is to be expected. But the laws of the banal, phillistine world do not hold good for spiritual relationships. If we wish to understand the spiritual world we must accustom ourselves to think with other thought forms; we must be prepared to experience many quite surprising things. When, in our everyday consciousness, we read about Goethe, we may naturally feel impelled to say: "How I should like to have known him personally, to have shaken hands with him!" and so on. That is thoughtlessness, for there are laws according to which we are predestined for a certain epoch of the earth in which we can live. Just as we are preconditioned to stand a certain pressure of the air in our physical body, and therefore cannot rise above the earth beyond a certain height where the pressure is not agreeable, so is a man who is predestined for the twentieth century unable to live at the time of Goethe.

These were the things which, at the outset, I wished to bring forward about karma.

V

Dornach, March 1, 1924

IF we speak in detail about karma, we naturally must distinguish, in the first place, between those karmic events of life which come to a human being from outside and those which arise, as it were, within his inner being. A human being's destiny is composed of many and diverse factors. His destiny is dependent on his physical and etheric constitution. It is dependent on what the human being, according to his astral and ego constitution, can bring of sympathy and antipathy toward the outer world, what others, again, according to his constitution can bring to him as sympathy and antipathy. Moreover, the destiny of the human being depends on the most manifold complications and entanglements in which he finds himself involved on the path of life. All of this determines the human being's karmic situation for any given moment of time or as a totality for his whole life.

I shall now try to put together the total destiny of man out of these various factors. For that purpose we intend today to take our point of departure from certain inner factors in the human being; we intend to look at that factor which, in many respects, is really of cardinal and decisive importance,—that is to say, his inherent tendency toward health and illness, and that which then becomes effective as the basis for this tendency in his strength of body and soul with which he is able to fulfill his tasks.

If we wish, however, to judge these factors correctly, we must be able to see beyond many a prejudice that is contained in modern civilization. We must be able to enter more into the original nature of the human being; we must gain real insight into what it signifies that the human being, as far as his deeper nature is concerned, descends from spiritual worlds into physical earth existence.

Now, you know that what is summed up in the concept of heredity has today found its way, for example, even into the realm of art, of poetry. If any one appears in the world with certain qualities, people inquire first about heredity. Or if, for example, some one appears with a pre-disposition to illness, they ask: "What about the hereditary relationships?"

This question is, indeed, at the outset quite justifiable, but in their whole attitude toward these things, people today ignore the real human being; they completely ignore him. They do not observe what his true being is, how his true being unfolds. Naturally, they say in the first place that he is the child of his parents, the descendant of his forebears. Certainly, this can be seen. Even in his outer physiognomy; and still more, perhaps, in his gestures do we see the likeness to his ancestors emerging. But not only this; we see also how the human being has his whole physical organism as a product of what is given to him by his forebears. He carries this physical organism about with him, a fact which is pointed out very forcefully today.

People fail, however, to observe the following: When he is born, the human being has most assuredly, at the outset, his physical organism from his parents. But what is this physical organism which he receives from his parents? In that regard the man of modern civilization thinks fundamentally quite falsely.

When the human being has reached the time of change of teeth, he not only exchanges his first teeth for others, but this is also the moment in life when the entire human being—as an organization—is renewed for the first time. There is a thorough-going difference between what the human being becomes in his eighth and ninth year of life, and what he was in his third or fourth year. It is a decisive difference. What he was—as an organism—in his third or fourth year, he received through heredity. His parents gave him that. What comes into being in his eighth or ninth year is the result, in the highest degree, of what he himself has brought down from the spiritual world.

If we wish to indicate in outline the really fundamental facts, we must do it in the following way—shocking though it may be to modern mankind. We must say, the human being receives as he is being born something like a model of his human form. He receives this model from his forbears; they bestow upon him a model. Then, aided by this model, he develops what he becomes later. What he then develops, however, is the result of what he brings down with him from the spiritual worlds.

Shocking as it may be to human beings of today, if they are completely immersed in modern culture, we must, nevertheless, make the following assertion: The first teeth which the human being receives are entirely inherited; they are the products of heredity. They serve him as a model according to which he fashions his second teeth in conformity to the forces he brings with him from the spiritual world. These he elaborates.

And as it is with the teeth, so is it with the body as a whole. Only, this question might arise: Why do we human beings need a model? Why can we not do just what we did in earlier phases of earth evolution? Why is it not possible as we descend and draw toward ourselves our ether body—which we do, as you know, with our own forces brought with us from the spiritual world,—why is it not possible likewise simply to gather to ourselves physical matter, and without the help of physical forbears form our own physical body?

To the modern human being's way of thinking, this question is obviously an example of monumental stupidity, an example of insanity. But then, we must indeed say that with respect to the insanity of the above statement, the Theory of Relativity holds good, although it is applied today only to movement, postulating, as it does, that we cannot tell from observation whether we are moving together with the body on which we find ourselves or whether it is the nearby body which is moving. (This fact became clearly evident in the exchange of the ancient cosmic theory for the Copernican.) But, although at present the Theory of Relativity is applied only to movement, it holds good—for it has a certain sphere of validity—it holds good also in regard to the aforesaid insanity: namely, here are two people who differ greatly; each one thinks the other crazy; the only question is,—which of the two is actually crazy.

Well, in relation to the facts of the spiritual world this question must, nevertheless, be raised: Why does the human being need a model? Older world conceptions have given the answer in their own way. Only in modern times, when morality is no longer included in the cosmic order, but is admitted solely as a human convention, are such questions no longer asked. More ancient world conceptions have not only asked these questions; they have even answered them. Originally, they said, the human being was so constituted that he was able to establish himself on the earth in the following manner: Just as he now draws to himself his ether body out of the general cosmic ether substance, so did he draw to himself the substances of the earth to form his physical body. But he fell a prey to the Luciferic and Ahrimanic influences, and as a result, he lost the faculty of building his physical body out of his own essential being. He must now receive it through heredity.

This way of obtaining the physical body is, for the human being, the result of "original sin," hereditary sin. This is what ancient world conceptions said. This is the fundamental meaning of "original sin," hereditary sin—the necessity of inserting oneself into the relationships of heredity.

In our age, the concepts must be provided again in order, first, to take such questions seriously, and secondly, in order to find the answers. It is a fact that the human being in his earthly evolution has not remained as strong as was his predisposition before the Luciferic and Ahrimanic influences were present. Therefore he cannot form his physical body through his own capacities as soon as he enters the earthly conditions, but he needs a model, that model which grows during the first seven years of human life. Since he conforms to this model, it is but natural that something of the model, more or less, remains with him in his later life. The human being who, working on himself, is completely dependent on the model will forget—if I may put it so—what he actually brought down with him and will entirely conform to the model. Another human being who has acquired stronger inner force through his former earth lives will conform less to the model, and it will be possible to see how significantly he changes in the second phase of life, between the change of teeth and puberty.

The school will even have the task, if it is a true school, to bring about in the human being the unfoldment of what he has brought into physical earth existence out of the spiritual worlds. Hence, what the human being carries further with him in life contains the inherited characteristics in greater or lesser degree, according as he is able or is not able to overcome them.

Now, just remember, my dear friends, that all things have their spiritual aspect. What the human being possesses as his body in the first seven years of life is simply a model to which he conforms. Either his spiritual forces are to some extent submerged in what is forced upon him by the model and he remains quite dependent on the model, or he works into the model during the first seven years of life that which will transform the model. This work, this elaboration, finds expression outwardly. For it is not merely a question that work is done and that this here (see Figure VI) is the original model; but the original model gradually detaches itself, peels off, so to speak, falls away, just as the first teeth fall out. Everything falls away. The matter is as follows: From one side, the forms and forces press upon the model; on the other, the human being wills to express what he has brought down to the earth. That causes a battle during the first seven years of life. Seen from the spiritual standpoint, this battle signifies what comes to outward symptomatic expression in the illnesses of childhood. The diseases of childhood are the expression of this inward struggle.

Figure VI

Needless to say, similar forms of illness occur in human beings later in life. That is the case if, for example, someone did not succeed very well in overcoming the model during the first seven years of life. Then the impulse may emerge later in life to get rid of what has thus karmically remained in him. Thus, in his twenty-eighth or twenty-ninth year of life, the human being may suddenly feel inwardly aroused against the model; he will only then collide with it and, as a result, fall prey to some illness of childhood.

If one has an eye for it, one can observe how strongly the following appears in many children: they change essentially in physiognomy and gesture after the seventh or eighth year of life. No one knows whence certain things come. Today, when the prevailing view of civilization adheres so strongly to heredity, this has even passed over into our way of speaking. If, in the eighth or ninth year, some feature suddenly emerges in a child which is deeply rooted in the organism, the father may say: "Anyhow, he did not get that from me," while the mother may say: "Well, most certainly not from me." All this is due to the common belief which has found its way into the parental consciousness that the children must have inherited everything from their parents.

On the other hand, it may often be observed how children grow even more like their parents in this second phase of life than they were previously. Here we must take in full seriousness the way the human being descends into the physical world.

Please note that Psycho-Analysis has, indeed, produced many really horrible swamp flowers; among them, for example, is the following—this may be read today everywhere—namely, that in the hidden, subconscious mind, every son is in love with his mother and every daughter with her father, and that this condition causes life conflicts in the subconscious provinces of the soul.*

All these are amateurish interpretations of life. The truth, however, is that the human being is in love with his parents already before he descends into earthly existence, that he descends because they please him. Only, we must naturally distinguish the judgment which people have here on earth about life from the judgment they have about it outside the earthly life between death and a new birth.

On one occasion, in the early stages of our anthroposophical activity, a lady appeared among us who had heard of reincarnation. She liked other things in Anthroposophy very much indeed, but in repeated earth lives she would not participate; one earth life was quite enough for her—with others she would have nothing to do. Now, at that time there were already very well-meaning adherents among us who tried in every possible way to convince the good lady that the idea was, after all, a correct one, and that every human being must participate in repeated earth lives. One friend belabored her from the left, and another from the right. She then departed, but two days later she wrote me a post card to the effect that, after all, she did not intend to be born again on earth!

In such a case, the one who wishes simply to tell the truth out of spiritual knowledge must say to people: "Certainly, it may be that, while you are here on earth, it is not at all to your liking that you should come down again to earth in some future life. But that is by no means decisive. Here on earth, you go through the gate of death into the spiritual world. You are willing to do this. Whether or not you wish to descend again depends on the judgment which will be yours when you no longer carry your body about with you. Then you will form quite a different judgment." The judgments a human being has in physical life on earth are different in every way from those he has between death and a new birth. For there every point of view changes.

These are the facts. If you tell a human being here on earth—a young human being, perhaps—that he has chosen his father, he might object under certain circumstances and say: "Do you mean that I chose the father who has beaten me so badly?" Yes, certainly, he chose him; for the youth had quite another point of view before he came down to earth.

* Cf. Rudolf Steiner: *Psycho-Analysis in the Light of Anthroposophy* (in preparation).

He then had the point of view that the thrashings would do him much good . . . This is, indeed, no laughing matter, it is meant in the deepest earnestness. In the same way a man also chooses his parents according to their form and figure. He has a picture of himself before him—the picture that he will resemble his parents. He does not become like them through heredity, but through his own inner soul and spirit forces, the forces he brings down with him from the spirit world. The moment, therefore, that we come to an all-inclusive opinion out of spiritual science as well as physical science, such wholesale statements are without exception no longer valid, for instance, the assertion: "I have seen children who became more like their parents only in the second phase of their life." Certainly, that is then just the other case, where these children intended to take on for this earth life the form of their parents.

Now it is a fact that the human being, during the whole time between death and a new birth, works in union with other departed souls and with the beings of the higher worlds upon that which makes it possible for him to build his body.

You see, we generally underestimate greatly the importance of what a man carries in his subconscious nature. As earth men, we are far wiser in the subconscious than in the conscious nature. It is, indeed, out of a far-reaching, universal, cosmic wisdom that we elaborate that which becomes within the model during the second phase of life the form that we then bear as our own human nature, the one that belongs to us. If, at some future time, we become aware of how little we really absorb, as far as the substance of the body is concerned, from the food we eat, how we take in far more from all that we absorb in a very finely diluted condition from the air and light, then we shall more readily be able to believe that the human being builds up his second body for the second life period quite independently of all hereditary conditions; he builds it entirely out of his environment. The first body is, actually, only a model. That which comes from the parents—as substance as well as the outer bodily forces—is no longer there in the second phase of life.

In the second life period the child's relationship to his parents becomes an ethical, a soul relationship. Only in the first period of life, that is, up to the seventh year, is it a physical, hereditary relationship.

Now, there are human beings in this earthly life who take a keen interest in all that surrounds them in the visible cosmos. There are men who observe the plants, observe the animal world; they enter with interest into this or that thing in the visible world around them. They take an interest in the majesty of the star-studded heavens. They take part, so to speak, with their souls in the entire physical cosmos. The inner life of a human being who has this warm interest in the physical cosmos differs from the inner life of one who passes the world by with a certain indifference, with a phlegmatic attitude of soul.

In this respect, we have a whole scale of human characters. On the one side, for example, there is a man who has taken a very short journey. When we talk to him afterwards, he describes with infinite love the city in which he has been, down to the minutest detail. Through his keen interest we may thus gain a complete picture of the city he had visited. From this extreme we can pass to the opposite,—to such as the instance, when I encountered two elderly ladies who had just travelled from Vienna to Pressburg. Pressburg is a beautiful city. They had returned, and I asked them what it was like in Pressburg, how they had liked it. They could tell me nothing except that they had seen two pretty little dachshunds down by the riverside. These they could have seen just as well in Vienna, they need not have gone to Pressburg for that purpose. But they had seen nothing else. Thus do many people go through the world.

Between these two extremes of the scale, there lies, indeed, every kind and degree of interest which the human being can have for what is in the physically visible world. Let us suppose some one has little interest for the surrounding physical world. It may be that he just manages to interest himself in the things that immediately concern his bodily life—whether, for instance, one can eat more or less well in this or that district. Beyond that his interests do not go. His soul remains poor. He does not imprint the world on himself. And he carries in his inner life very little of what has radiated toward him from the phenomena of the world through the gate of death over into the spiritual realms. Because of this he finds the work with the spiritual beings, with whom he now comes into contact, very difficult. And, in consequence, he brings back in his soul not strength, not energy, but feebleness, a kind of powerlessness for the upbuilding of his physical body. The model, to be sure, works strongly upon him. The fight with the model finds expression in the manifold illnesses of childhood; but the weakness persists. He forms, so to speak, a frail or sickly body, subject to all manner of illnesses. Thus, our soul-spirit interest from one earth life is transformed karmically into the state of health in the next life. Human beings who are "bursting with health" had a keen interest in the visible world in a former incarnation. And in this regard, the details of life act very powerfully.

It is certainly more or less risky nowadays to speak of these things. But we shall understand the relationships of karma only if we are ready to occupy ourselves with the details about it. The art of painting, for example, already existed at a time when human souls, now living, were living in a former earth life; and there were human beings who had no interest at all in painting. Even today there are people who are quite indifferent whether they have some atrocity hanging on the walls of their room, or a well-painted picture. And there were also such people at the time when the souls who are living today were present in former earth lives. Indeed, my dear friends, I have never found a human being with a pleasing face, a sympathetic expression, who did not take delight in the art of painting in a former earth life. The people with an unpleasing expression (which, after all, also plays its part in karma and has its significance for destiny) were always those who had passed by the works of the art of painting with obtuse and phlegmatic indifference.

But these things go much farther. There are human beings (and there were also such in former epochs of the earth) who never look up at the stars, who do not know where Leo is, or Aries, or Taurus, who have no interest in anything in this connection. Such people will be born, in a subsequent earth life, with a body that is somehow indolent; or, if through the vigor of their parents they receive a model which carries them beyond this, they become flabby, lacking in energy and vigor in the body which they then build for themselves.

And thus it is possible to trace back the state of health which the human being bears with him in a given earth life to the interest he had taken in the visible world to the widest extent during his former earth life.

People, for instance, who in our time take absolutely no interest in music—people to whom music is a matter of indifference—will certainly be born again in a next earth life with asthmatic trouble, or with some disease of the lungs; or, they will be born with a susceptibility to asthma or lung disease. It is an actual fact that the quality of soul which develops in one earth life through the interest we take in the visible world comes to expression in our next earth life in our general bodily disposition in regard to health or illness.

Perhaps, some one might now say: "To know of such things may well take away one's taste for the next earth life." That, again, is a judgment pronounced from the earthly standpoint, my dear friends, which is certainly not the only one; for the life between death and a new birth lasts longer than the earth life. If a man is obtuse to something visible in his environment, he remains incapable of working in certain realms between death and a new birth, and he has passed, let us say, through the gate of death with the consequences of this lack of interest. After death, he proceeds on his way. He cannot get near certain beings; certain beings hold themselves apart from him, for he cannot approach them. Other human souls with whom he was associated on earth remain strangers to him. This would go on for ever; there would be something like a punishment in Hell for eternity, if this could not be modified. The only cure, the only compensation, lies in his resolving—between death and a new birth—to come down again into earthly life and feel in a sick body that which is an incapacity in the spiritual world. Between death and new birth he desires this cure, for he lives with awareness of but one thing, namely, that there is something he cannot do; but he feels this in such a way that in the further course of events, when he dies again, and again passes through the time between death and a new birth, that which was earthly pain becomes the impulse to enter into what he missed the last time. Thus we may say that in all essentials, we carry with our karma health and disease out of the spiritual world down into the physical.

And if we bear in mind in this connection that it is not always a karma in course of fulfillment, but also a karma in process of becoming, so that certain things may also appear for the first time, then we shall naturally not relate to the former earth lives of a human being everything he experiences in his physical life as regards health and illness. That which, with its roots in the inner nature, appears in regard to the conditions of health and illness, is, we shall know, karmically determined in the roundabout way I have just characterized. The world becomes explicable only when we are able to look beyond this earthly life. Without this the world is inexplicable; it cannot be explained by means of the earth life.

If from the inner conditions of karma, which ensue from the organism, we now pass on to what is external, toward the outer, we may once more—only in order, at the outset, to come in contact with karma, as it were—we may once more proceed from a realm of facts which touches the human being closely. Let us take, for example, that which can be very strongly connected with the general mood of soul health and illness in our relationship with other human beings.

I should like to offer the following case: Some one finds a friend in his youth. An intimate friendship of youth is formed; the two friends are very devoted to one another. Life separates them, so that both of them, perhaps—or, perhaps, one especially—look back with a certain sadness to this youthful friendship. But it does not permit of renewal. However often they meet in life, their friendship of youth is not again renewed. If you consider how much in destiny can sometimes depend on such a broken friendship of youth, then you will admit that this sort of thing can profoundly affect a person's karma.

We should speak as little as possible about such things out of mere theory. To speak out of theory has very little value. In truth, we should speak of such things only from direct perception or else on the basis of that which we have heard or read in the communications of those who are able to have direct perception and which appears plausible to us and is comprehensible. There is no value in theorizing about these things. Therefore I say, when you endeavor with spiritual perception to get behind such an event as a broken friendship of youth, the following results: If we go back into a former earth life, we usually find that both individuals who in one life had a friendship in their youth which was afterwards broken, were in an earlier incarnation friends in the later part of their life.

Let us assume, for instance, two young people—boys or girls—are friends until their twentieth year. Then the friendship of their youth breaks. If we go back with spiritual cognition into a former earth life, we find there that a friendship also existed, but it had begun around the twentieth year and continued on into later life. That is a very interesting case, which we often find when we follow up things with spiritual science.

In the first place, when we examine the case more exactly, it appears that the urge to know a person also as he was in youth with whom we had a friendship in our mature years leads us in the next life to a youthful friendship with him. In a former life we knew him as a mature human being. That brought into our soul the urge to become acquainted with him also in youth. This we could no longer do in that life, so we carry it out in the next life.

But that has a great influence if in one or both of these individuals this urge arises, passes through death, and then lives itself out in the spiritual world between death and a new birth. For there is then something present in the spiritual world like a fixed staring at the period of youth. We have this quite special longing to fix our gaze on the time of youth, and we do not develop the urge to become acquainted with our friend once more in his maturity. Thus the youthful friendship is broken which was predetermined between us by the life we had lived through before we came down to earth.

This is decidedly a case which I recount to you out of real life, for what I am now relating is absolutely real. The question, however, arises here: What was the mature friendship really like in the former life, so that it caused this urge to arise to have the human being as a friend again in youth in a new earth life?

Now, in order that the impulse to experience this youthful friendship does not, however, increase into a wish to have the friend also in later life, something else must occur. In all the instances of which I am aware, the following has invariably been the case: If these two human beings had remained united in their later life, if their youthful friendship had not

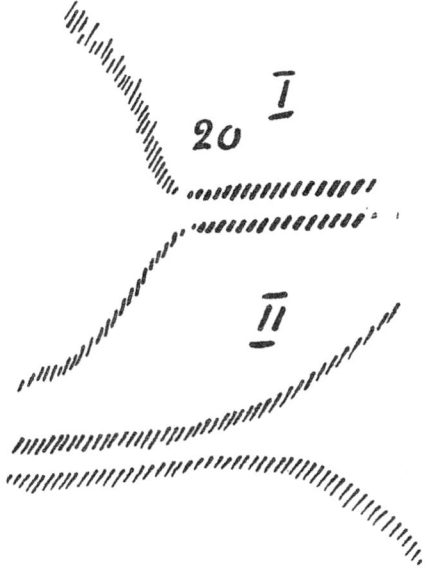

Figure VII

been broken, they would have grown tired of each other, bored with one another, because their friendship which occurred in maturity in a former life developed too egotistically. The egotism of friendships in one earth life avenges itself karmically by the loss of these friendships in other earth lives.

Thus, things are complicated; but we can always find a guiding line if we see the following: It is a fact in many cases that two human beings in one earth life—let us say—go each his own way until their twentieth year, and thenceforward continue on together in friendship (see Figure

VII, No. I). In a subsequent earth life, this picture (I) corresponds to another (Figure VII, No. II), the picture of the youthful friendship after which their lives separate. This is very frequently the case. Indeed, it will generally be found that the various earth lives—seen, as it were, according to their configuration—mutually supplement each other. Especially is the following frequently found to be true. If we encounter a human being who has a strong effect upon our destiny—this applies, naturally, only as a general rule; it is not applicable in all cases—but if we meet an individual

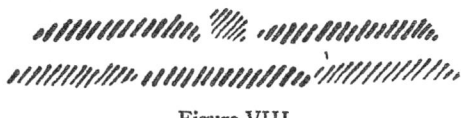

Figure VIII

in the middle period of life in one incarnation, we have had him beside us perhaps at the beginning and at the end of life in a prior incarnation in accordance with destiny. The picture is then as follows: We live through the beginning and the end of one incarnation together with the other human being, and in another incarnation we live with him neither at the beginning nor at the end, but we only encounter him in the middle period of life.

Or again, it may be that as a child we are bound by destiny to another human being; in a former life we were linked to the same individual just before we experienced death. Such reflections occur with extreme frequency in karmic relationships.

VI

Dornach, March 2, 1924

IN continuing our studies on karma, we are under the necessity, at the outset, of casting a glance at the manner in which karma intervenes in the evolution of man, how destiny, which intervenes with the free deeds of man, is really fashioned in its physical reflection out of the spiritual world.

To begin with, I shall have to tell you today a few things about that which is connected with the human being in as far as he lives on earth. This earthly man—during these lectures we have been studying him in regard to the various members of his being. We have distinguished in him the physical body, the ether body, the astral body, the ego organism. We can, however, by directing our gaze upon him, just as he stands before us in the physical world, perceive the membering of the human being in yet another way.

Today we intend—quite independently of what we have already been discussing—to consider a certain membering of the human being, and we shall try to build a bridge between what we discuss today and that which we already know.

If we consider the human being as he stands before us on the earth, simply according to his physical form, then this physical form has three clearly differentiated members. This differentiation is, however, not usually observed, because that which asserts itself as science nowadays really looks at things and facts in a merely superficial way. It has no sensibility for what reveals itself when things and facts are considered with a perception inwardly illumined.

We have, to begin with, the human head. Even outwardly considered, this human head shows itself as something quite different from the remainder of the human form. We need but turn our attention to the formation of the human being out of the human embryo. The first thing we can see developing in the body of the mother as human embryo is the head organization.

The whole human organization takes its start from the head, and everything else in the human being which afterwards flows into his configuration is, actually, an appendage-organ of the human embryo. As physical form, the human being is a head in the beginning. The rest are appendage-organs. And the functions which these appendage-organs assume in later life—such as breathing, circulation, nutrition—are, in the first period of the embryonic existence, activities proceeding not from within the embryo, but from without inward, out of the body of the

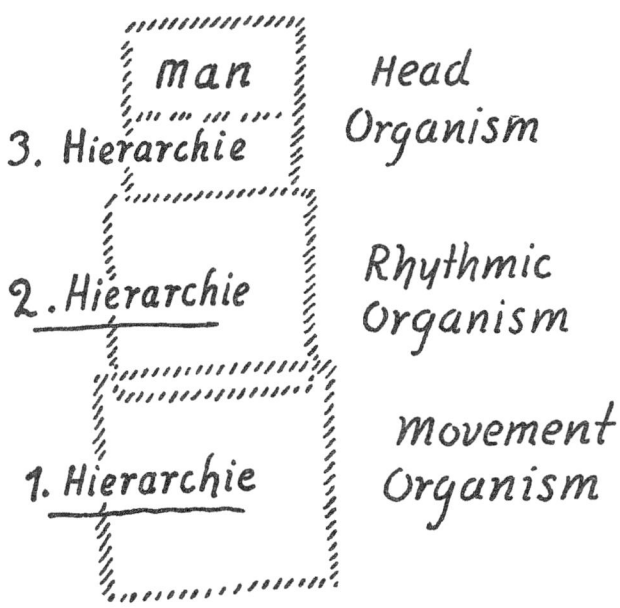

Figure IX

mother, through organs which afterwards fall off, organs which are no longer present later in the human being.

The human being is, at the outset, entirely head. The rest is appendage-organ. We do not exaggerate in the following sentence: The human being is in the beginning head; the rest is, so to speak, appendage-organ. Since that which at first was appendage-organ later on grows and gains in importance for the human being, his head finally loses its sharp distinction from the rest of the organs.

But this gives only a superficial characterization of the human being.

For in reality he is, also as physical form, a threefold being. All that which actually constitutes his first form—the head—remains throughout his earthly life a more or less individual member. We fail merely to recognize this; nevertheless, it is a fact.

You will say: Indeed, one ought not to divide the human being in such a way that we behead him, as it were, chop off his head. That this happens in Anthroposophy was only the belief of Professor "Blank" who reproached Anthroposophy for dividing men into head, chest organs, and limb organs. But this charge is not true; it is not at all a fact; for in what is outwardly head configuration lies only the main outer expression of the head configuration. Man remains completely "head" throughout his whole life. The most important sense organs—the eyes, ears, the organs of smell, the organs of taste—are, to be sure, in the head, but the sense of warmth, for example, the sense of pressure, the sense of touch, are spread out over the whole human being. That is precisely because the three members of the human organism are not to be differentiated spatially, but only in such a way that the head formation mainly appears in the outwardly formed head, while in reality it permeates the entire human being. And this is true also for the rest of the members. The head is, throughout man's earthly life, in the big toe, in so far as the big toe possesses a sense of touch or a sense of warmth.

Thus we have characterized, to begin with, the one member of the human being's essential nature, that human nature which confronts us as something sensuous. In my books I have designated this organization also as the nerve-sense organism in order to characterize it more inwardly. This, then, is one member of the human being, the nerve-sense organism.

The second member of the essential nature of the human being is all that manifests in rhythmical activity. You cannot say of the nerve-sense system that it finds expression in rhythmic activity, for example, in the perception of the eye; for in that case you would have to perceive one thing at a certain moment, then another, then a third, then a fourth, and then return again to the first, and so on. In other words, there would have to be a rhythm in your sense perception. But that is not the case. Observe on the other hand the main characteristic of your breast organism. There you will find the rhythm of breathing, the rhythm of circulation, the rhythm of digestion, and so forth. There, everything is rhythm.

Rhythm, with its organs of rhythm, is the second thing to develop in the human being; and it also extends over the whole human being, though its chief external manifestation is in the organs of the breast. The whole human being, again, is a lung; yet lung and heart are localized, so to speak, in the organs so named. The whole human being, indeed, breathes; you breathe in every spot of your organism. People speak of skin respiration. Only, in the activity of the lung is respiration mainly concentrated.

The third human organism is that of the limbs—the limb organism. The limbs terminate in the breast organism. In the embryonic stage of existence they appear as appendages. They are the latest to develop. They are, however, the organs which are chiefly connected with metabolism. The metabolic process finds its chief stimulus through the fact that these organs are put into motion, perform most of the work in the human being. We have thus characterized the three members that appear to us in the human form.

But these three members are intimately connected with the soul life of the human being. His soul life can be divided into thinking, feeling, and willing. Thinking finds its physical expression chiefly in the head. But it has its physical organism also in the entire human being, because the head exists, in the way I have just described, throughout the entire human being.

Feeling is connected with the rhythmic organism. It is a prejudice, indeed even a superstition on the part of modern science to assume that the nervous system has directly to do with feeling. The nervous system has nothing directly to do with feeling. The respiration and circulation rhythms are the organs of feeling, and the nerves only transmit the fact that we cognize our feelings, that we experience them. The feelings have their organism in the rhythmic system, but we should know nothing of our feelings if the nerves did not procure for us percepts of them. And because the nerves procure for us these percepts of our feelings, modern intellectualism creates the superstition that the nerves themselves are the organs of feeling. This is not the case.

But, when we consciously observe our feelings, as they arise out of our rhythmic organism, and compare them with the thoughts which are bound to our head, to our nerve-sense organism, then—if we are able to observe at all—we shall perceive the same difference between our thoughts and our feelings that exists between our daytime thoughts which we have in waking life and our dreams. Our feelings have no greater intensity in consciousness than dreams. They only have a different form; they only make their appearance in a different way. When you dream in pictures, your consciousness lives in pictures. But these pictures, in their picture character, have the same significance—although in another form—as our feelings. Thus we may say that we have the clearest consciousness, the most illumined consciousness in our visualizations, in our thoughts. We have a kind of dream consciousness in regard to our feelings. We only believe that we have a clear consciousness of our feelings; we have no clearer consciousness of our feelings than we have of our dreams. If on awaking from sleep we recollect our dreams and form of them wide-awake visualizations, we do not seize hold of the dream. The dream is far richer than our visualization of it afterwards. In like manner is the world of feeling infinitely richer than our mental pictures of it, which we make present to our consciousness.

And completely immersed in sleep is our willing. This willing is bound to the limb-metabolic organism, to the motor organism. All that we really know of our willing are the thoughts. I form the visualization: I shall take

Figure X

hold of this watch. Just try to think quite sincerely that you form the visualization: I shall take hold of this watch. Then you do take hold of it. What proceeds from your visualization, your thought, right down into the muscles and finally leads to something which again appears as a visualization—your taking hold of the watch, which is a continuation of the first visualization—what lies between the thought of the intention to act, and the thought of its fulfilment, what occurs in your organism, all these activities remain just as unconscious as your life in the deepest dreamless sleep.

We do at least dream of our feelings, but from our impulses of will we have nothing but what we have from our sleep. You may say: I have nothing at all from sleep. Well, I do not speak now from the physical standpoint; even from the physical standpoint it is, indeed, entirely senseless to say that you have nothing at all from sleep. But psychically, too, you have a great deal from your sleep. If you were never to sleep, you would never reach your ego consciousness.

You need only realize the following: When you remember the experiences you have had, then you say that you are going back in time, that from the present you go further back in time. Indeed, you imagine that it is a fact that you go further back in time. But it is not so at all. In reality you only go back to the moment when you awoke from sleep the last time. (See Fig. X.) Then you have fallen asleep. What lies there between is eliminated. And then in the interval from the last time you fell asleep back to the time before the last when you woke up, memory appears again. So the matter continues on, back in time. And by looking back, you must really always insert the periods of unconsciousness. In doing so we must insert unconsciousness for one third of our life. We do not pay attention to this. But it is just as if you had a white plane with a black hole in the center. (See Fig. XI.) You see the black hole, in spite of the fact that there are no forces present. Thus, in looking back in memory, in spite of the fact that it contains nothing from life's reminiscences, you see, nevertheless, the blackness—the nights, through which you have slept. There

Figure XI

your consciousness strikes against this blackness continually, and that impels you to call yourself an I, an ego.

If this really continued on and you were to knock against nothing, you would never gain an ego consciousness. Thus we can, indeed, say that we benefit from sleep. And just as we benefit from our sleep in the ordinary earth life, do we benefit from the sleep which rules in our willing. We sleep through that which really takes place in us with every act of will. But in it there lies the true ego. Just as we receive our ego consciousness through the black void (see Figure XI), so does our ego lie in that which sleeps in us during the act of will—the ego, however, which passed through our former earth lives.

That is where karma holds sway. Karma rules in our willing. In our willing all the impulses from our preceding earth life hold sway; only, even in the waking human being, they are sunk in sleep.

Thus, when we visualize the human being as he confronts us in earth life, a threefold membering of his organism is observable: the head organism, the rhythmic organism, and the motor organism. That is a schematic division. Each member belongs in turn to the whole man. Visualizing is bound to the head organism, feeling is bound to the rhythmic organism, and willing to the motor organism. Our state while visualizing is wakefulness, while feeling is dreaming. Our state in which willing, in which the will impulses take place is sleep, even during our waking life.

Now, in the head—that is, in our visualizing—we must distinguish two things; we must discover, as it were, a more subtle membering of the head. This more subtle membering leads us to distinguish what we have as momentary visualization by virtue of our having intercourse with the world, from what we have as memory.

You go through the world, constantly forming visualizations, mental images, according to the impressions you receive from the world. But it remains possible for you to call up these impressions again out of your memory. The visualizations you form in your intercourse with the world at present are not differentiated inwardly from the visualizations aroused to life when memory becomes active. In one case they come from without, and in the other from within. It is, indeed, a naive thought to imagine that memory works in the following way: I now confront a thing or event, form a visualization, a mental picture of it; this visualization sinks down into me somewhere, into some sort of pigeon-hole, and, when later I remember, I take it again out of the pigeon-hole. There are, indeed, whole philosophies which are able to describe how the visualizations sink down beneath the threshold of consciousness, then are fished out again in the act of recollecting. These are naive concepts.

There is, of course, no such pigeon-hole in which our visualizations lie when we remember them. Nor is there any such place in us where they are moving about and whence, when we remember them, they walk up again into our head. All these things are utterly non-existent, nor is there any explanation in their favor.

The facts are rather as follows, you need only to reflect on the following: When you wish to exercise your memory, you often do not work merely with your powers of visualizing, but you bring to your aid very different means. I have seen people memorizing who exercised their power to visualize just as little as possible, but carried on vehement outer movements accompanying their speech (arm movements) again and again:

And it undulates, surges, and roars and hisses*

* *Und es wallet und woget und brauset und zischt.*
A well-known line of German poetry. (Tr.)

Thus people memorize in this way, and in so doing the least possible thinking occurs. And in order to add a further stimulus—*And it undulates, surges, and roars and hisses*—they beat their forehead with their fists. Even this happens. It is definitely a fact that the visualizations we form as we occupy ourselves with the world are as evanescent as dreams. On the other hand, what emerges out of memory are not visualizations which have sunk below into us, but something quite different. Were I to give you some notion of it, I should have to draw it thus (see Figure XII). This is, naturally, only a kind of symbolic figure. Imagine the human being as a seeing being. He sees something. I shall not describe the process more exactly; that could be done, but for the moment we do not need it. The human being sees something. It passes through his eye (see Figure XII), through the optic nerve into the organs into which the optic nerve then merges.

We have two clearly distinct members of our brain: the more external brain, the gray matter; and, beneath it, the white matter. The white matter terminates in the sense organs, the gray matter lies within it; it is far less developed than the white mass. "Gray" and "white" are, of course, only approximate terms. But even thus crudely anatomically considered, the matter is as follows: The objects make an impression on us, pass through our eyes, and on into the processes that take place in the white matter of the brain.

On the other hand, our visualizations have their organs in the gray matter (see Figure XII) which, incidentally, has quite a different cell structure. Therein our visualizations glimmer and vanish like dreams. They glimmer, because the impressions are occurring underneath.

If you were dependent upon having the mental images sink down into you, and you then had to call them up again in memory, you would remember nothing at all, you would have no memory. The fact is like this: At the present moment, let us say, I see something. The impression of it—whatever it may be—sinks into me, the white matter of the brain acting as the medium. The gray matter functions by dreaming in its turn of the impressions, making pictures of them. These are only transitory pictures; they come and go. That which remains we do not visualize at all at this moment, but that goes down into our organism. And when we remember, we look within; down there below, the impression remains.

Thus, when you see something blue, then an impression of blue sinks down into you (below, in Figure XII), here (above, in Figure XII) you form the visualization of blue. It is transitory. Then, after three days, you observe in your brain the impression which has remained. Now, by looking inward, you visualize the blue. The first time, when you saw the blue from without, you were stimulated from outside by the blue object. The second time, when you remember, you are stimulated from within, because the blueness portrayed itself within you. In both cases, the process is the same. It is always a perception. Memory, too, is a perception. So that our day-waking consciousness is actually to be found, as it were, in the visualizing process; but, beneath the visualizing, certain processes are going on which also rise into consciousness through visualizing, namely, through the memory visualizations. Below this visualizing lies perceiving,

Figure XII

the actual perception, and only below this lies feeling. Thus we can distinguish more intimately between the processes of visualizing and perceiving in our head organism, our thought organism. That which we have perceived we can then remember. But it remains, indeed, very unconscious; only in memory does it rise into consciousness. What really takes place in the human being is actually no longer experienced by him. When he perceives, he experiences the visualization. The effect of the perception penetrates him. Out of this effect he is able to awaken the memory. But then the unconscious has already begun.

In reality it is only here, in this region—where in waking-day consciousness we visualize—there only do we ourselves exist as human beings. There only are we really aware of ourselves as human beings (see Figure

XIII). Where we do not reach down with our consciousness (we do not even reach the causes of our memories) there we are not aware of ourselves as human beings, but are incorporated into the world. It is just as it is in the physical life. You inhale, the air you now have within yourself was a short while ago outside, it was the air of the outer atmosphere; it is now your air. After a short time you give it back again to the world; you are one with the world. The air is now outside you, now inside you, now without, now within. You would not be a human being were you not united with the world in such a way that you possess not only that which is

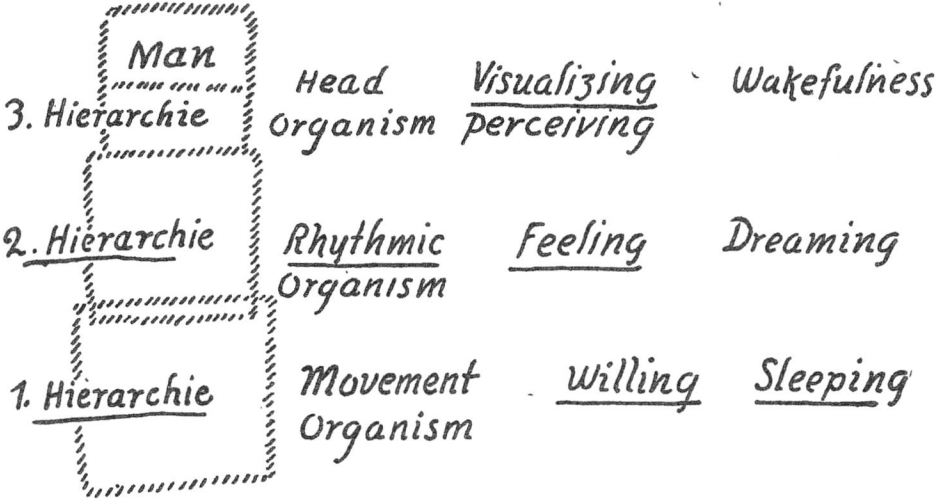

Figure XIII

present within your skin, but that by means of which you yourself are connected with the whole surrounding atmosphere. And just as you are thus connected on your physical side, so are you connected on your spiritual side—the moment you descend into the nearest sub-conscious region, the region out of which memory arises—so are you connected with that which we call the third Hierarchy, Angeloi, Archangeloi, Archai. Just as you are connected through your breathing with the air, so are you connected through your head organism, the lower head organism, with the third Hierarchy. The outer lobes of the brain, consisting of gray matter, only and solely belong to the earth. What is beneath (the white matter) is connected with the third Hierarchy, Angeloi, Archangeloi, Archai.

Now let us descend into the region, psychologically speaking, of feeling; corporeally speaking, of the rhythmic organism, out of which the dreams of our feeling life arise. There we do not at all possess ourselves as human beings; there we are connected with what constitutes the second Hierarchy—the spiritual beings who do not incarnate in any kind of earthly body, but who remain in the spiritual world. They, however, send unceasingly their currents, their impulses, that which streams from them as forces, into the rhythmic organism of the human being. Exusiai, Dynamis, Kyriotetes—these are the beings whom we bear within our breast.

Just as we bear our human ego only in the outer lobes of our brain, so do we bear the Angeloi and Archangeloi, directly beneath this region, but still within the head organism. That is the scene of their earthly activities; there the starting-points of their activity are to be found.

In our breast we bear the second Hierarchy—Exusiai, and so forth; there in our breast are the starting-points of their activity. And if we now descend into the sphere of our motor organism, if we enter our movement organism, then in this sphere the beings of the first Hierarchy are active—Seraphim, Cherubim, Thrones.

The transmuted food-stuffs, the food-stuffs we have eaten, circulate in our limbs, undergo there a process which is a living combustion process. For, if we take just a single step, there arises in us a living process of combustion, a burning up of that which was outside us. We are connected with it. Through our limb and metabolic organism, we are connected as human beings with the lowest, and yet it is precisely through the limb organism that we are connected with the highest. With the first Hierarchy, with the Seraphim, Cherubim, Thrones, we are connected by that which permeates us with spirit. Now the great question arises—it may sound trivial in that I clothe it in earthly words, but there is nothing else I can do—the question arises: With what are they occupied—these beings of the three successive Hierarchies, while they are among us—with what do they occupy themselves?

The third Hierarchy—Angeloi, Archangeloi, and so forth—concerns itself with that which has its physical organism in the head; this Hierarchy occupies itself with our thinking. Were it not concerned with our thinking, with that which takes place in our head, we would have no memory in ordinary earth life. The beings of this Hierarchy retain in us the impulses which we receive with our perceptions. They underlie the activity which manifests itself in our recollection, manifests itself in memory. They lead us through our earth life within this, our first unconscious region.

Now let us proceed to the beings of the second Hierarchy—Exusiai, and so forth. They are the beings we encounter when we have passed through the gate of death, in the life between death and a new birth. There we encounter the souls of the departed human beings who lived with us on earth; but we encounter there, above all, the spiritual beings of this second Hierarchy—also, it is true, those of the third Hierarchy, but the second Hierarchy is more important. We work with them during the time between death and a new birth upon all that we have felt in our earth life, all that we have transplanted into our organism. In union with these beings of the second Hierarchy, we elaborate our next earth life.

When we stand here on the earth, we have the feeling that the spiritual beings of the divine world are in us. When we are there beyond in the sphere between death and a new birth, we have the reverse thought. The Angeloi, Archangeloi and so forth, who guide us through our earth life in the manner indicated, live on the same plane with us, so to speak, after our death. Directly underneath are the beings of the second Hierarchy. With them we work on the forming, the shaping, of our inner karma. And all that I told you yesterday about the karma of health and disease we elaborate with these beings, the beings of the second Hierarchy.

And if we look still deeper in the time between death and a new birth, that is, if we, as it were, look through the beings of the second Hierarchy, then below we discover the beings of the first Hierarchy, Cherubim, Seraphim, and Thrones. As earthly human beings, we seek the highest Gods above us. We seek as human beings between death and a new birth in the profoundest depths below us for the highest Divinity attainable by us. And while we are working with the beings of the second Hierarchy, elaborating our inner karma between death and a new birth, that inner karma which afterwards appears reflected in the healthy or diseased constitution of our next earth life, while we are engaged in this work, while we work with ourselves and with other human beings upon the bodies which will then appear in our next earth life, the beings of the first Hierarchy are occupied below in a peculiar way. We behold that. They stand within a certain necessity in regard to their activity, in regard to a part, a small part, of their activity. They must imitate—for they are the creators of the earthly—that which the human being has molded during his earth life, but imitate it in a quite definite way.

Think of the following: In his will, the human being performs certain deeds on earth. The will belongs to the first Hierarchy. Be these deeds good or bad, wise or foolish, the beings of the first Hierarchy—Seraphim,

Cherubim, Thrones—have to mold the counterparts of these deeds in their own sphere.

You know, my dear friends, we live together. No matter, whether the things we do together are good or evil, for all that is good, for all that is evil, the beings of the first Hierarchy must shape the corresponding counterparts. Among the first Hierarchy all things are judged, but also shaped and fashioned. While we work on our inner karma with the second Hierarchy and with the departed human souls, we behold between death and a new birth what Seraphim, Cherubim, and Thrones have experienced through our earthly deeds.

Indeed, my dear friends, here upon earth the blue sky with its cloud formations and sunshine arches over head, and at night, as the starry heavens, it vaults above us. Between death and a new birth the activity of the Seraphim, Cherubim, and Thrones vaults beneath us. And we gaze down upon these Seraphim, Cherubim, and Thrones just as we here look up to the clouds, to the blue heaven, to the star-strewn heaven. Beneath us we behold the heavens formed of the activity of Seraphim, Cherubim, and Thrones. But what kind of activity is it? While we live between death and a new birth, we behold the Seraphim, Cherubim, Thrones performing the activity which results as the just and compensating activity from our own deeds on earth—our own and the earthly deeds lived through with other human beings. The Gods are obliged to exercise the compensating activity, and we behold it as our heavens which are now beneath us. In the deeds of the Gods we behold the consequences of our earthly deeds, whether good or bad, wise or foolish. And by looking downward we relate ourselves, between death and a new birth, to the reflection of our deeds in the same way as in earthly life we relate ourselves to the vaulting heaven above us.

We carry our inner karma into our inner organism. We bring it back with us onto the earth as our faculties and talents, our genius and our stupidity. What the Gods fashion there beneath us, what they must experience in consequence of our earth lives, confronts us in our next earth life as the facts of destiny which come to meet us from without. We may say that what we pass through to which we are asleep carries us into our destiny in our earth life. But in this lives what the Gods in question, those of the first Hierarchy, had to experience as the consequences of our deeds in their domain during the time between our death and a new birth.

One always feels the need of expressing such things in pictures. Let us imagine ourselves standing somewhere in the physical world. The sky is overcast; we behold the clouded sky. Soon thereafter, a rain begins to trickle down; the rain is falling. What previously hovered above us we now see on the dripping fields, on the dripping trees. If we look back, with the eye of the initiate, from human life into the time we passed through between our last death and our last birth, we then see therein, first of all, the forming of divine deeds, the consequences of our own deeds in our last earth life. We then see how this spiritually rains down and becomes our destiny.

If I meet a human being who has significance for me in earth life, who has a determining influence upon my destiny, what occurs with this meeting of the other human being has been previously experienced by the Gods as a result of what I have had in common with him in a former earth life. If I am transferred during my earth life to some locality important to me or placed in some important calling, all that comes to me thus as outer destiny is a likeness of what the Gods have experienced—Gods of the first Hierarchy—as a consequence of my former earth life, during the time when I was myself between death and a new birth.

Indeed, if you think abstractly, then you think: "There we have the former earth lives; the deeds of the former earth lives work across into the present. Previously they were causes; now they are effects." With this we cannot think very far; we have actually little more than words when we make this statement. But behind what we thus describe as the law of karma lie the deeds of the Gods, experiences of the Gods; and behind all that lie the other facts.

If we human beings approach our destiny only through feeling, then we look up, according to our faith, either to the Gods or to some Providence, upon which we feel the course of our earth life depending. But the Gods—those whom we know as the beings of the first Hierarchy, Seraphim, Cherubim, and Thrones—have, as it were, a reverse religious confession. They feel their necessity lies with men on earth whose creators they are. The aberrations human beings suffer, and the progress they enjoy, must be equalized by the Gods. And what the Gods prepare for us as our destiny in a subsequent life they have already lived through before us.

These truths must be found again through Anthroposophy. Out of a consciousness not fully developed, they were perceived by mankind in an erstwhile instinctive clairvoyance. The ancient wisdom contained such truths. Then only a dim feeling about them remained. In much that meets us in the spiritual life of mankind, there is still a dim feeling for these things. You need only remember the verse by Angelus Silesius which you will also find quoted elsewhere in my writings. To a narrow religious understanding it sounds like an impertinence:

> *Without me, God could not a moment live at most.*
> *Came I to naught, must He from need give up the ghost.* *

Angelus Silesius went over to Roman Catholicism and as a Catholic wrote such verses. To him it was still clear that the Gods are dependent on the world, just as the world is dependent on the Gods, that this dependence is something mutual, and that the Gods must direct their life according to the life of human beings. But the divine life acts creatively, and has its effect in turn in the destiny of human beings. Angelus Silesius, dimly feeling, but not knowing the exact truth, said:

> Without me, God could not a moment live at most.
> Came I to naught, must He from need give up the ghost.

World and Godhead depend on one another and work into one another. Today we have seen this interactivity in the example of human destiny, of *karma*.

* *Ohn' mich könnt' Gott ein Nu nicht leben.*
Würd' ich zunicht, müsst' er vor Not den Geist aufgeben.

www.ingramcontent.com/pod-product-compliance
Lightning Source LLC
Chambersburg PA
CBHW022122040426
42450CB00006B/810